GW01071896

and for fish. Beyond the Accademia, you can walk over to the Zattere and watch the big ocean-going vessels push aside the *vaporetti* (water buses) and little *motoscafi* (water taxis). On the point of the lagoon, the wonderful domed Baroque church of Santa Maria della Salute awaits your visit: for too many people it remains just a romantic landmark on the skyline. In fact it contains a superb Tintoretto and other fine paintings by Titian.

In the other direction is Veronese's delightful church of San Sebastiano, his burial place and veritable museum for some of his finest work. If your taste happens to be more modern, right near to the Accademia is the Palazzo Venier dei Leoni housing the magnificent collection of 20th-century art of the Peggy Guggenheim Foundation.

The artistic choice is endless: Titian's great altarpiece in the Frari church, the monumental series of paintings by Tintoretto in the venerable guild of Scuola di San Rocco, the series by Carpaccio in the guild of the Schiavoni (Dalmatians).

And So Much More

Take time, too, for a closer look at the façades of palaces which the Venetians, with characteristic false modesty, often preferred to call houses *(Ca')*: the exquis-

ite Gothic Ca' d'Oro and Ca' Foscari, or the superb Baroque Ca' Rezzonico. Children love the grotesque masks on Palazzo Pesaro.

Of the islands out in the estuary, Murano is famous for its glassware, Burano for its lace and Torcello for its beautiful cathedral. The Lido has the old-fashioned elegance of a classical seaside resort, fine sandy beach, casino, luxury hotels. Rent a bicycle and explore it from end to end.

For many, Venice is a non-stop festival—Mardi Gras carnival with fantastic costumes and masks, the formidable summer Biennale, avant-garde festivals of fine arts, music and theatre, and in September, the film festival. Venice's churches provide a magnificent setting for concerts, notably the organ recitals at St Mark's. Opera at La Fenice has always counted among the finest in Europe, and when fire destroyed the interior of the theatre in 1996, no time was wasted in finding an alternative. Until restoration is completed (scheduled for 1998), performances are held in the PalaFenice tent set up on Tronchetto. Mozart's *Don Giovanni,* the opera that so epitomizes the spirit of the town, is known as a *dramma giocoso,* in other words, a playful drama. That's Venice.

Flashback

Reluctant Beginnings

They didn't want to go there, but the barbarians left them no choice. In ancient times, the lagoon was just a place for coastal dwellers to go fishing around the little islands and extract salt for winter food-storage. Then, as the Roman Empire crumbled, successive waves of invaders drove them off the Adriatic coast to seek shelter in the offshore archipelago. First came the Goths in 402, then Attila and his Huns 50 years later. As soon as the dust of pillage had settled, many of the refugees moved their homes back to the mainland.

But increasingly, as the raids grew more frequent, people stayed behind to make more permanent communities out of their island settlements. In their flat-bottomed barges, the lagoon people prospered, already, by trading surplus goods around the waterways of central and northern Italy. After the invasion in 568 of the Lombards who, unlike the hit-and-run Goths and Huns, had clearly come to stay, the people of the lagoon formed a solid confederation of communities calling themselves collectively the Venetiae.

In 697, the Venetians chose a doge (local dialect for the Latin *dux*) to head their provincial government, initially answerable to the Byzantine emperor in Constantinople. Installed on Malamocco island out by the Lido, Orso was the first of an unbroken line of 118 doges that lasted 1,100 years. (A spurious portrait in the Doges' Palace council chamber wrongly identifies the first doge as Paoluccio Anafesto, who was in fact head of the church at Ravenna.) In 774, the Venetians withstood attack by an army of Franks led by Charlemagne's son, Pépin, but were forced to move their capital to Rivo Alto (Rialto), the island of the present Doge's Palace and Piazza San Marco. (Malamocca disappeared in a tidal wave in 1107.)

Republic Rules the Waves

Masterful shipbuilding and brazen trading methods marked Venice's rise to riches and power in the Middle Ages. Ignoring the strictures of Constantinople and Rome, the city traded with Muslims in lumber, salt and, above all, slaves. With Arab gold, the Venetians bought Oriental silks and spices from Constantinople for resale in western Europe at huge profits. In times when merchants habitually moonlighted as pirates, the fast and sturdy Venetian fleet gradually won control of the Adriatic from their ruthless but undisciplined Dalmatian rivals. In 1000, Doge Pietro Orseolo II celebrated the Republic's domination by tossing a diamond ring into the water in a ritual "wedding to the sea", which became an annual tradition. Venice extended its maritime supremacy across the eastern Mediterranean and borrowed Levantine styles in the sumptuous architecture of the 11th-century basilica of San Marco, the city's patron saint.

From 1095, the Crusades proved a boon to the city's treasury. The Venetians became high priced charter-travel agents and even higher priced arms manufacturers for the mission to "save" the Holy Land. Never letting religion interfere with business, Venice required the European armies to earn their passage by knocking off the Republic's trade rivals on their way to Palestine. On the Fourth Crusade (1202–1204), the French and Flemish soldiers never even got there. After a first stop-over to massacre Venice's enemies on the Croatian coast, the knights were shipped straight to Constantinople. With the promise of fabulous riches in this capital of the eastern Christian empire, the knights went on a ferocious rampage of plunder, rape and murder. By Doge Enrico Dandolo's prearranged plan to secure control of the eastern Mediterranean, Venice put its own man on the imperial throne—and got the lion's share of the booty to pay for the trip.

The brutality of the stratagem won the hatred of eastern and western Christendom alike, but it carried the Republic to the zenith of its power and the merchants of Venice cried all the way to the bank.

Tough at the Top

In the late 13th century, adding prudence to their audacity, the Venetians decided that their empire was now too big for one man. The doge was reduced to a purely ceremonial role, a majestic bird in exotic plumage wandering around the gilded cage of his palace. The Great Council of 1,000 aristocrats entrusted governmental decisions to a Council of Ten.

In the Mediterranean, Venice had to fight it out with mighty Genoa for control of Cyprus, Crete and other Greek islands. They also competed for the Black Sea's lucrative markets in grain and slaves, or the spices-

8

FLASHBACK

for-cloth trade in London, Bruges and Antwerp. It was Venetian and Genoese cargoes from the Crimea that brought the plague-bearing rats and the Black Death of 1348 to western Europe. Venice lost half its population in just over a year. But it was still able to muster enough courage and resources to throw back the last but most menacing of the Genoese attacks, right at the gateway to the lagoon in 1379.

The success tempted Venice to over-extend its power. In the 15th century, besides gobbling up more major ports around Greece and Albania, it moved onto the Italian mainland and provoked Milan, Naples and Florence into forming a hostile alliance. At sea, a more serious threat arose with the Turkish conquest in 1453 of Constantinople, irrevocably weakened by the Venetian-led destruction 250 years earlier. The Republic lost a vital battle at Negroponte (modern Khalkis on the Aegean island of Euboea) in 1470 and gave up more key trading counters to the Ottoman Turks along the Adriatic and Aegean coasts over the next 30 years.

At the same time, the exploits of two navigators knocked the commercial wind out of Venice's sails in the Mediterranean. In 1492, Christopher Columbus turned eyes to the riches of the Americas. Six years later, Portugal's Vasco da Gama ended Venice's virtual monopoly of the spice-trade by opening up a new route to India around Africa's Cape of Good Hope.

The Golden Decline

Back home, the town's era of greatness was being immortalized by its artists and scholars. Just as the religiously devout were drawn to the Holy Places of Jerusalem, so profane pilgrims— the first tourists—flocked to Venice to see the architecture of Jacopo Sansovino and Andrea Palladio and the paintings of Giovanni Bellini, Giorgione, Carpaccio, Titian, Veronese and Tintoretto. They proved to be the Republic's most brilliant beacons before its power began to wane.

Throughout the 16th century, the popes and Emperor Charles V whittled away at Venice's holdings on mainland Italy. The Republic knew a brief moment of glory in 1571 when its fleet played a leading role in the Holy League's prestigious victory over the Turks at Lepanto, but at the same time it lost the strategic eastern Mediterranean outpost of Cyprus. In ending the myth of Turkish invincibility, Venice was also relegated from the league of great powers.

9

Set off on foot to explore Venice: serendipitous surprises await around every corner.

The native talent Venice had previously devoted to conquering overseas markets was now given over to the gentler art of good living. The quality of its new textiles, glassware and book printing, and its time-honoured commercial know-how ensured a less spectacular but still comfortable income. Having survived its turbulent centuries on the world stage without the ravages of foreign invasion, the town's palaces and churches remained splendidly intact. While any self-respecting young gentleman's Grand Tour of 18th-century Europe would inevitably include the august cities of Florence, Rome and Athens, Venice was considered the most enjoyable of all, whether for the finesse of the operas and concerts of Monteverdi and Vivaldi and the theatre of Goldoni, or for the more outrageous pleasures of the Carnival. Never was a brothel more elegant than when set in a Baroque palazzo on the Grand Canal.

Tears of Grief and Joy

Napoleon Bonaparte put a bitter end to the glittering Venetian adventure. His French forces conquered all of Venice's territories on the mainland, and an ultimatum demanded total surrender. On May 12, 1797, exactly 11 centuries after the election of the first doge, the 118th and last, Lodovico Manin, tearfully abdicated as the Great Council voted to dissolve the Most Serene Republic. Had they not done so, Bonaparte would probably have carried out his threat of being an "Attila" for the city on the lagoon. As it was, carefully guided by French art experts, his troops plundered the treasures of the palaces and churches. Taken from the monastery of San Giorgio Maggiore, Veronese's monumental *Wedding Feast of Cana*, along with two other paintings of the master from the Doge's Palace, still hang in the Louvre. As a supreme humiliation, the soldiers burned the *Bucintoro*, the grandiose galley from which the doge performed his wedding ceremony with the sea.

In the 19th century, Venice was ruled by the Austrian Habsburgs. They brought back many of the artistic treasures looted by the French and, for the first time, linked the city to the mainland by a railway built in 1846. Venetians joined the European wave of revolt of 1848 and drove out the Austrian troops, but independence was short-lived as the Habsburgs re-established their authority for another 17 years. In a plebiscite following the Prussian victory over Austria in 1866, the Venetians finally threw in their lot with the rest of Italy, voting to join the new kingdom.

Keeping Afloat

Since then it has been content, more or less, to become a glorious backwater. And water has remained a major preoccupation as successive administrations and world experts sponsored by UNESCO fight to keep the city from sinking into the lagoon or being eaten away by pollution.

Henry James set his *Portrait of a Lady* and *Wings of the Dove* in Venice, while Thomas Mann, of course, immortalized it in *Death in Venice*. The international film festival on the Lido, the first such in the world, was the brainchild of Benito Mussolini—and one of the few lasting cultural benefits that Italy gained from his rule. An international playground—and workshop—for the rich and famous, the town welcomed Ernest Hemingway, who settled a while on the island of Torcello, writing between drinking bouts in Harry's Bar, and Peggy Guggenheim, who installed her great modern art collection in the Palazzo Venier dei Leoni.

For the rest of us mere mortals, it is still the place where lovers come to mend a broken heart—or break a whole one.

11

Landmarks

Venice is a sparkling mosaic of 120 islands separated by some 180 canals and joined by more than 400 bridges. Its magnificent palaces and churches are supported on millions of wooden piles driven into the muddy bottom of the lagoon.

GRAND CANAL

All visitors to Venice have to follow the Grand Canal to reach their final destination. There can be nothing more delightful than gliding past the ribbon of Byzantine, Gothic, baroque, Renaissance and neoclassical palaces and historic buildings which adorn both banks of the Canalazzo from the Piazzale Roma or Santa Lucia Station all the way to San Marco, opposite the Dogana da Mar. For a more detailed description of historic buildings along the Grand Canal, see pp. 26–28.

PIAZZA SAN MARCO

The religious and political centre of Venice, Saint Mark's Square is lined on three sides by splendid palaces. On the north side are the Procuratie Vecchie, dating from the 12th century, originally the headquarters of the "procurator" of Saint Mark's and nowadays used as offices. On the south side are the Procuratie Nuove, and on the east side the Ala Napoleonica, whose façade is crowned with statues of Roman Emperors.

BASILICA DI SAN MARCO
Piazza San Marco
In summer, open daily
9.45 a.m.–5 p.m., Sunday 2–5 p.m.
In winter, open daily
10 a.m.–4 p.m., Sunday 2–4 p.m.
A basilica of great beauty and harmony, despite the different styles that have been superimposed since its foundation in the 9th century—Byzantine, Gothic and Renaissance. Left of the basilica is the Piazzetta dei Leoni, named after the two handsome red marble lions which date from 1722.

CAMPANILE DI SAN MARCO
Piazza San Marco
Open daily 10 a.m.–4 p.m.
Almost 100 m (330 ft) high, this bell-tower is one of the first things you notice as you approach the city. The existing tower was completed in 1912, its 12th-century predecessor having collapsed in 1902. A lift whisks you to the top in a few seconds for a wonderful view of Venice and the Adriatic.

PALAZZO DUCALE
Piazzetta San Marco
Open daily 8.30 a.m.–5 p.m.
Nine hundred years old, this palace was the residence of the doges. It was rebuilt in the 14th-century in the Gothic style and became the symbol of the government of the Republic of Venice.

TEATRO LA FENICE
Campo San Fantin 1965,
San Marco
Closed for restoration until 1998.
In January 1966 a fire destroyed the interior of the sumptuous Venice Opera House, mourned the world over. Only its classical façade was spared by the flames.
(See PalaFenice, p. 50.)

TORRE DELL'OROLOGIO
Mercerie dell'Orologio, San Marco
Built between 1496 and 1499, the
tower is surmounted by the Moors,
two bronze figures which strike the
hour on a large bell. The clock face
marks the hours in Roman and
Arabic numerals and with the signs
of the Zodiac. Unfortunately, it is no
longer possible to climb the 136
steps to inspect the Moors from
close at hand.

PALAZZO ALBRIZZI
Campiello Albrizzi, San Polo
Visits on request.
A little off the beaten track, this
palace has a beautiful late-16th-
century façade. The interior is richly
decorated.

SCUOLA GRANDE
DI SAN GIOVANNI EVANGELISTA
Campiello della Scuola 2454,
San Polo
Visits by appointment (tel. 718 234).
The *scuole* (schools) were meeting
places for lay confraternities formed
by groups of citizens who shared a
common origin or profession.
This school was built between the
14th and 18th centuries and the
different styles are clearly visible
on the façade.
The interior has two rooms where
you can admire paintings by
Tintoretto, Tiepolo and others.

GONDOLAS
The gondola is practically synony-
mous with Venice. These distinc-
tive boats have been negotiating
the canals since the 11th century.
In olden days, wealthy Venetians
used to paint their gondolas in
bright colours and decorate them
richly. Rivalry among the nobles as
to who had the finest gondola
reached such a point that in 1562
the government enacted a new
law decreeing that all gondolas
must be painted black, and they
have stayed black to the present
day. Until the 19th century there
were some 10,000 gondolas on the
canals, but now only 500 remain,
usually used to transport tourists
around the city. Before you let
yourself be punted away, agree on
a price with the gondolier.

SCUOLA GRANDE
DI SAN ROCCO
Campo di San Rocco 3054,
San Polo
Open daily 10 a.m.–4 p.m.
Four successive architects built
this school, but they managed to
keep a certain harmony in their
additions to the façade.
Inside you can see over fifty works
by Tintoretto; some claim
that this collection of paintings
counts among the three best in the
whole of Italy.

SCUOLA GRANDE DEI CARMINI
*Campo dei Carmini,
Dorsoduro
Open daily 9 a.m.–noon and
3–6 p.m. Closed Sunday.*
This was the headquarters of the
prestigious confraternity founded in
1594 and dedicated to the Virgin of
Carmel; it became extremely
powerful after about a hundred
years of existence. The edifice has
two different façades. The interior
has retained its original appearance
with rich ceilings and many
paintings from the 17th and 18th
centuries (Tiepolo, Piazzetta).

CA' D'ORO
Cannaregio 3933
The Ca' d'Oro palace ("Golden
House"), nowadays presenting a
façade of marble lace, takes its name
from its once-gilded exterior.
Built in the Gothic style between
1422 and 1440, it has undergone
alterations several times over the
centuries. It houses the Franchetti
Gallery (see p. 24).

PALAZZO LABIA
*Campo di San Geremia,
Cannaregio
Visits by appointment
(tel. 524 28 12)*
One of the most ostentatious of the
17th–18th century palaces, with
huge rooms decorated with Tiepolo

frescoes. It is now the headquarters
of RAI (Italian television).

ARSENALE
Campo dell'Arsenale, Castello
The imposing gate of the Arsenal
(off-limits to tourists!) opens onto
this *campo*. High walls surrounded
by natural and artificial canals
enclose the complex of docks,
factories and warehouses which
built the Venetian fleets, the basis
of the economic, political and
military power of the Republic.

PALAZZO GRIMANI
Ruga Giuffa 4854, Castello
Completed in 1569, this palace used
to house the Greco-Roman
collection which is now part of the
Archaeological Museum. The
gateway leads to a historic
courtyard.

SCUOLA DI SAN GIORGIO DEGLI SCHIAVONI
*Calle dei Furlani, Castello
Open daily (except Monday)
10 a.m.–12.30 p.m. and 3–6 p.m.*
The Schiavoni Confraternity (from
Dalmatia) founded this school,
dedicated to Saints Giorgio and
Trifone, in the 15th century. It has
important paintings by Vittore
Carpaccio and, on the first floor, a
collection of other works from the
mid-17th century.

Churches

In front of each church there is a campo or small square, sometimes bordered by canals and enclosed by dwellings, and often creating a private and secret world. The only piazza in Venice is the great square in front of Saint Mark's Basilica.

Churches are generally open from 9 or 10 a.m. until noon, and from 4 or 5 p.m. until 7 p.m.

SAN MOISÈ
Campo San Moisè,
San Marco
Founded in the 8th century and rebuilt several times before the 17th century, this church has a Venetian-baroque façade.

SAN SALVADOR
Campo San Salvador,
San Marco
Of ancient origin, this church has been restored over and over again. The interior has three aisles, and is rich in important works of art.

SANTO STEFANO
Campo F. Morosini,
San Marco
One of the major Gothic edifices of the city. The interior is huge: it has three aisles and a magnificent wooden ceiling.

SAN ZULIAN
Campo San Zulian,
San Marco
An old church founded in 829. Many works of art in the interior.

SAN GIACOMO DI RIALTO
Campo San Giacomo di Rialto,
San Polo
This is the oldest church in Venice (5th–6th century). It still has its original door and interior medieval columns complete with capitals.

SAN POLO
Campo San Polo
Originally a Byzantine church, it was altered in the 15th century. It contains paintings by Tintoretto, Palma the Younger and Tiepolo.

SAN ROCCO
Campo San Rocco, San Polo
Begun in 1489, this church is consecrated to Saint Rocco, who was believed to offer protection against the plague. The saint is shown in bas-relief on the façade, the work of the sculptor Morlaiter.

Inside, several paintings by Tintoretto illustrate episodes from the life of the saint, who was born in Montpellier, France.

SANTA MARIA GLORIOSA DEI FRARI
Campo dei Frari, San Polo
The 70-m (230-ft) high bell-tower is the highest in Venice after San Marco. The church, both severe and grandiose, is a memorial to 500 years of La Serenissima's glorious history and culture. Titian's *Assumption* is its most famous work of art, but others by Bellini and Donatello are also of note.

SAN GIACOMO DELL'ORIO
Campo San Giacomo dell'Orio,
Santa Croce
The date of its foundation is unknown, but the church was rebuilt in 1225. The interior has all the charm of a medieval building and some admirable works of art.

SAN NICOLÒ DA TOLENTINO
Campo et Campazzo dei Tolentini,
Santa Croce
Standing in this interesting *campo* which gives onto a *rio* (a small canal), the church (c.1600) retains rich decoration added in the 18th century.
Many works of art by Palma the Younger, Luca Giordano and others.

SAN STAE

Campo San Stae, Santa Croce
Rebuilt in the 17th century in
Palladian style, this church is used
for temporary exhibitions and
concerts.

SANTA MARIA MATER DOMINI

*Campo Santa Maria Mater Domini,
Santa Croce*
A Renaissance-style church with a
simple and elegant interior, adorned
with admirable works by Vincenzo
Cateno and Tintoretto.
The *campo* is one of Venice's most
characteristic squares, thanks to its
regular shape and pleasing
proportions, and to the magnificent
Byzantine and Gothic buildings
which surround it. Note the 13th-
century Casa Zane (No. 2174), Casa
Viaro-Zane (Nos. 2120–22) and the
14th century Casa Barbaro
(No. 2177).

I GESUATI

*Fondamenta Zattere ai Gesuati,
Dorsoduro*
Built between 1724 and 1736 with
donations from the inhabitants of
Venice, this church is the happy
result of collaboration by the
greatest artists of the 18th century.
The interior is a veritable gallery for
the sculptor Giovanni Maria
Morlaiter, and there are works by
Tiepolo. Piazzetta and Tintoretto.

SAN NICOLÒ DEI MENDICOLI

*Campo San Nicolò dei Mendicoli,
Dorsoduro*
The origins of this church go back to
the 7th century. The porch, which
used to be a shelter for the poor, is
typical of this period.

SAN PANTALON

*Campo San Pantalon,
Dorsoduro*
An important church as early as the
11th century, it is celebrated for the
40 canvases by Giovanni Antonio
Fumiani which cover the ceiling of
the nave, illustrating the martyrdom
and glory of San Pantaleone.
Other works to be seen are by Paolo
Veronese and Palma the Younger:
there is a splendid *Coronation of the
Virgin* by Antonio Vivarini and
Giovanni d'Alemagna.

SAN RAFFAELE ARCANGELO

*Campo Angelo Raffaele,
Dorsoduro*
This church built in the form of a
Greek cross was reconstructed
between 1618 and 1639. It houses
16th and 17th century art works. The
paintings by Antonio Guardi are
exceptional.

SANTA MARIA DEL CARMELO
(I CARMINI)

*Campo dei Carmini,
Dorsoduro*

A church which has been enlarged and altered several times since the 14th century. Inside, many important works by Cima da Conegliano, Giorgio Martini and Lorenzo Lotto.

SANTA MARIA DELLA SALUTE
Campo della Salute, Dorsoduro
This church is recognized to be the supreme achievement of Longhena's baroque architecture. He built it between 1631 and 1687. A solemn festival dedicated to the Virgin is celebrated here annually.

GESUITI (SANTA MARIA ASSUNTA)
Campo dei Gesuiti, Cannaregio
Built by the Jesuits (c.1730), this church in the form of a Latin cross and with a beautiful baroque façade, became first a school and then a barracks when the order was disbanded in 1773. Important paintings by Titian and Tintoretto embellish the interior.

GLI SCALZI (SANTA MARIA DI NAZARETH)
Fondamenta degli Scalzi, Cannaregio
This church was begun in 1654 and built to a design by Longhena for a community of Discalced (barefooted) Carmelites. The decoration is similar to Roman baroque; the façade is the only one in Venice to be made of Carrara marble. Paintings by Tiepolo.

MADONNA DELL'ORTO
Campo della Madonna dell'Orto, Cannaregio
A 14th-century church rebuilt or altered in the 15th century and adorned with statues on its magnificent terracotta façade. The interior, bathed in light from the upper windows, has three aisles. Tintoretto is buried in this church, which possesses many of his paintings.

SANT'ALVISE
Campo Sant'Alvise, Cannaregio
The charm of this church of 1388 resides in the contrast between its rustic exterior and the sumptuous interior decoration, enriched by Tiepolo paintings.

SAN GIOBBE
Campo San Giobbe, Cannaregio
Rebuilt in Gothic and finished in Renaissance style, this church is famous for the sophisticated decoration of the portal and the interior vaulting. The second chapel on the left is superb. It contains the only example in Venice of the work

19

of the Della Robbia, a ceiling covered in terracotta with polychrome varnish.

SAN GIOVANNI CRISOSTOMO

Salizzada San Giovanni Crisostomo, Cannaregio

An elegant bell-tower dominates the simple Renaissance façade of this church rebuilt between 1497 and 1504. Among its many works of art there is an altarpiece by Sebastiano del Piombo, *Saint John Chrisostome with other Saints* (1509).

SAN MARCUOLA

Campo San Marcuola, Cannaregio

The vast, incomplete façade of this church rises from one of the rare *campi* opening directly onto the Grand Canal. It was renovated between 1728 and 1736. See the remarkable 18th-century statues on the chapel altars and a splendid *Last Supper* by Tintoretto.

SANTA MARIA DELLA MISERICORDIA (SANTA MARIA VALVERDE)

Campo dell'Abbazia, Cannaregio

The little square in front of the church, with its original terracotta paving, retains all the charm of bygone times. The church itself was built with the adjoining abbey in the

10th century and rebuilt in the 13th century. It subsequently underwent several alterations.

PIETÀ (SANTA MARIA DELLA VISITAZIONE)

Calle della Pietà, Castello

Built between 1745 and 1760, it has an elegant nave designed for concerts, a luminous fresco by Tiepolo on the ceiling and a vast entrance designed to cut out external noise.

SAN FRANCESCO DELLA VIGNA

Campo San Francesco della Vigna, Castello

The grandiose façade was completed between 1564 and 1570 to a blueprint by Palladio. The bell-tower, similar to that of San Marco, is one of the tallest in the city. Inside there is an altarpiece (1562) by Veronese.

SAN GIORGIO DEI GRECI

Ponte dei Greci 3412, Castello

This church belonged to the Greek Orthodox community, the biggest foreign community living in Renaissance Venice. Dignified and harmonious, it is rich in Byzantine paintings and icons. The elegant bell-tower stands next to the façade.

SAN GIOVANNI IN BRÀGORA

Campo della Bràgora, Castello

The primitive 8th-century church was rebuilt in the 9th century when the supposed relics of Saint John the Baptist were brought from the Orient. The building you see today dates from the 16th century. The Gothic interior has works by Cima da Conegliano, Bartolomeo and Alvise Vivarini.

SAN ZACCARIA

Campo San Zaccaria, Castello

The 12th-century Romanesque church was rebuilt in 1490 in Renaissance style. The interior is a charming mingling of different styles. Huge canvases cover the walls, but the masterpiece is an altarpiece by Giovanni Bellini, *The Holy Conversation*.

SANTA MARIA FORMOSA

Campo Santa Maria Formosa, Castello

According to tradition, this church was raised in 639 by Saint Magno and rebuilt several times afterwards. Note the grimacing head which surmounts the entrance to the bell-tower. The *campo* is one of the largest in the city, enlivened by a small market and some very busy cafés. It is surrounded by palaces dating from various periods.

SANTA MARIA DEI MIRACOLI

Campo dei Miracoli, Castello

This small isolated church is one of the earliest and happiest examples of Venetian-Renaissance architecture, like a jewellery box set with precious polychrome marble. It was built to enshrine an image of the Virgin which had become an object of great veneration. The interior reproduces the elegance of the exterior in its marble cladding.

SANTI GIOVANNI E PAOLO

Campo dei Santi Giovanni e Paolo, Castello

From the 15th century, the funerals of the Doges were always celebrated here. Together with the Frari, this church is the most grandiose example of Venetian-Gothic architecture, the pantheon of the city's glories. The walls contain the sepulchres of the Doges, some of exceptional artistic worth. The many chapels are adorned with magnificent works of art. The presence of the imposing Dominican monastery, the church and the adjoining Scuola Grande di San Marco, make this one of the most historic *campi* of Venice. Here stands the equestrian statue of Bartolomeo Colleoni (a captain who served the Republic for 21 years), a splendid Renaissance sculpture by Andrea Verrocchio.

Museums

A visit to a museum often brings the added bonus of seeing the interior of a sumptuous palace from a bygone age.

BIBLIOTECA NAZIONALE MARCIANA

Piazzetta San Marco 7
Visits by appointment Monday to Friday (tel. 520 87 88).

Endowed with more than 900,000 volumes and approximately 13,000 manuscripts, this library also houses the Grimani Breviary (late 15th century), one of Europe's most precious illuminated texts.

MUSEO ARCHEOLOGICO

Piazzetta San Marco 17
Open daily 9 a.m.–2 p.m.

Occupying several rooms in the Procuratie Nuove, this museum has an important collection of Greek sculpture, fragments of Roman sculpture and monuments, as well as Roman coins and marble statues. Many of the pieces were donated by humanist and theologian

Domenico Grimani and his nephew Giovanni in the 16th century.

MUSEO CIVICO CORRER
Piazza San Marco
Open daily 9 a.m.–5 p.m.
This museum is housed in the Ala Napoleonica and some rooms of the Procuratie Nuove. An interesting collection of art works, historical artefacts and documents relating to the Republic of Venice.

PALAZZO GRASSI
Campo San Samuele 3231, San Marco
Opening hours change according to exhibitions.
Major artistic events and special exhibitions are held in this imposing 18th-century building.

CASA GOLDONI
San Tomà, San Polo
Closed for restoration.
Once the home of Goldoni, the celebrated 18th-century dramatist, and now housing a museum and library.

GALLERIA D'ARTE MODERNA DI CA' PESARO
Fondamenta di Ca' Pesaro 2076, Santa Croce
Closed for restoration, but groups can visit by appointment (tel. 72 11 27).

This gallery occupies rooms in one of the most famous of Venetian palaces on the Grand Canal. It was founded in 1897 to display a series of works from the Biennale exhibitions, and now has one of the greatest collections of Italian and foreign paintings, sculptures and drawings from the end of the 19th century until the present day. Among the 20th-century artists represented here are Arp, Chagall, De Chirico, Ernst, Kandinsky, Klee, Klimt, Mirò and Moore.

MUSEO D'ARTE ORIENTALE
Fondamenta di Ca' Pesaro 2076, Santa Croce
Open daily (except Monday) 9 a.m.–2 p.m.
A large collection of Japanese art from the Edo period (1614–1868) and sections devoted to China and Indonesia.

MUSEO CIVICO DI STORIA NATURALE
Salizzada del Fontego dei Turchi 1730, Santa Croce
Closed for restoration.
This house in 13th-century Venetian-Byzantine style was originally an inn and warehouse for Turkish merchants. It now contains an unusual collection of fossils, mammals, minerals and marine fauna.

23

COLLEZIONE PEGGY GUGGENHEIM

Calle San Gregorio 701, Dorsoduro
Open daily (except Tuesday)
11 a.m.–6 p.m.

A prestigious collection of European and American avant-garde artworks in the Palazzo Venier dei Leoni, which was for 30 years the Venetian residence of the American collector Peggy Guggenheim.
The surrealist collection and the Jackson Pollock collection are particularly rich.

COLLEZIONE VITTORIO CINI

Piscina del Forner 864,
Campo San Vio,
Dorsoduro
Open during the summer months.

On two floors of a Renaissance palace, this is a collection of antique furniture, objets d'art and paintings of the Tuscan school from the 13th to 15th centuries (Daddi, Lippi, Piero della Francesca, Pontormo).

GALLERIE DELL'ACCADEMIA

Campo della Carità 1050, Dorsoduro
Open daily 9 a.m.–7 p.m.; public holidays 9 a.m.–2 p.m.

The biggest collection of Venetian art, begun in 1807 and housed in the old buildings of Santa Maria della Carità, which was a combined church, monastery and school. Among the artists represented are Bellini, Giorgione, Mantegna, Piero della Francesca, Lorenzo Lotto, Veronese, Tintoretto and Titian.

MUSEO DEL SETTECENTO VENEZIANO

Ca' Rezzonico, San Barnaba 3136, Dorsoduro
Open daily (except Friday)
10 a.m.–4 p.m.

An exceptional collection of paintings, objets d'art and furniture of the 18th century in one of the largest baroque palaces on the Grand Canal.

PINACOTECA MANFREDIANA

Campo della Salute 1, Dorsoduro
Visits by appointment
(tel. 522 55 58).

A collection of 15th–18th century paintings, hung in the rooms of the Seminario Patriarcale, a spacious palace by Longhena begun in 1671.

GALLERIA FRANCHETTI

Calle Ca' d'Oro 3933, Cannaregio
Open 9 a.m.–1.30 p.m.

Housed in the Ca' d'Oro and the neighbouring Palazzo Giusti, this collection boasts Italian and foreign paintings, marbles, bronzes and ceramics. As well as the famous

Saint Sebastian by Andrea Mantegna, there are important works by Titian, Tintoretto, Van Eyck, Guardi and Bellini.

MUSEO COMUNITÀ EBRAICA
Campo di Ghetto Nuovo 2902, Cannaregio
Open daily (except Saturday and on Jewish holidays)
10 a.m.–4.30 p.m. (Friday 4 p.m.).
Interesting examples of Venetian Jewish art of the 17th to 19th centuries, religious objects, tapestries and manuscripts.

BIENNALE INTERNAZIONALE D'ARTE
Giardini Pubblici, Castello
An important exhibition of contemporary painting, sculpture, graphic and decorative art, enjoying the participation of nations from all over the world.
Instituted in 1895, it takes place every odd-numbered year. Between 1907 and 1964, every participating country (about thirty all told) constructed a pavilion. The whole represents a fascinating museum of modern architecture.

MUSEO DELL'ISTITUTO ELLENICO DI STUDI BIZANTINI E POST-BIZANTINI
Eglise San Giorgio dei Greci, Ponte dei Greci 3412, Castello
Open daily except Sunday and public holidays 9 a.m.–12.30 p.m. and 2–4.30 p.m.
An exhibition of Byzantine and post-Byzantine icons, objects of worship and other sacred objects.

MUSEO STORICO NAVALE
Campo San Biagio 2148, Castello
Open daily (except Sunday and public holidays) 9 a.m.–1 p.m.
Old naval relics, trophies and scale models, principally Venetian. It includes the model of *Bucintoro*, the State galley of the Doges, and other Venetian vessels of the 18th century.

PINACOTECA QUERINI-STAMPALIA
Campiello Querini-Stampalia 4778, Castello
Open daily (except Monday) 10 a.m.–1 p.m. and 3–6 p.m. (Friday and Saturday 10 p.m.).
The second floor of the Querini-Stampalia palace holds a large collection of 14th–18th century works of art, with paintings by Palma the Younger, Luca Giordano and Giovanni Bellini.
The façade of the palace (1528) gives onto a charming little *campiello* beside the Santa Maria Formosa canal and follows the curve of its banks.

Out and About

It's a memorable delight to stroll through the campi (squares), campielli (small squares) and calli (streets and lanes) of this magical city, where more than nine buildings out of ten are historic monuments.

❑ GRAND CANAL

The most beautiful high street in the world, the Grand Canal meanders for two and a half miles through the city. Here, in order, are the principal historic buildings which line its banks.

A church and many palaces were destroyed in 1954 to make way for the Santa Lucia Station. The only survivor is the **Chiesa degli Scalzi**, a baroque church commissioned in 1654 from the architect Longhena by the Roman community of Discalced Carmelites (it means barefooted but the nuns and friars wore sandals). Before you pass under the Ponte degli Scalzi, look for the **Chiesa di San Simeon Piccolo** (18th century) crowned with a large copper dome.

On your right after the first bend in the canal you will see the **Fondaco dei Turchi,** an old Venetian-Byzantine palace which was a warehouse for Turkish merchants after 1621.

On your left, the Renaissance style **Palazzo Vendramin-Calergi** was the last home of the composer Richard Wagner. It is the winter quarters of the municipal Casino.

Look again to the right. Next to the **Chiesa San Stae,** founded in the 10th century and dedicated to St Eustace, there is a small building with a red façade which was once the headquarters of the guild of drawers and spinners of gold. A little further on, the imposing **Ca' Pesaro,** arguably the most handsome baroque palace in Venice, houses the museums of Oriental Art and Modern Art. The **Ca' Corner della Regina** dates from the 18th century and was built on the site of the house where Caterina Cornaro was born in 1454: she became the Queen of Cyprus upon her marriage to Jacques II of Lusignan.

The **Ca' d'Oro** (left bank), a delicate mingling of Byzantine and Gothic, contains the collections of Baron Franchetti, bequeathed to the Municipality in 1916.

You are now approaching the Rialto. The fish market is held each morning in the **Pescheria,** a square building in neo-Gothic style on the right bank. Follow the immense façades of the **Fabbriche nuove** and the **Fabbriche vecchie,** originally commercial buildings and today housing the Law Courts.

Standing on the left bank just before the Rialto Bridge, the **Fondaco dei Tedeschi** was a warehouse reserved for German traders, now the central Post Office. Along the left bank after the bridge, there is a series of prestigious palaces. The **Palazzo Dolfin Manin,** built in 1550, is today the head offices of the Bank of Italy. The **Palazzo Bembo,** with Gothic windows, dates from the 15th century. **Ca' Loredan** and **Ca' Farsetti,** both built in the 13th century, together form the Town Hall.

Almost opposite the Palazzo Grimani, a sumptuous Renaissance dwelling, the **Palazzo Papadopoli** (right bank) was constructed in the 15th century for a family of jewellers. Next door, the **Palazzo della Madonetta** has retained a pretty 15th-century bas-relief of the Virgin and Child.

Further along on the left, the **Palazzi Mocenigo,** a group of four

27

buildings in Istrian stone from the 16th and 17th centuries, provided inspiration for Lord Byron, who began work on Don Juan when he stayed here in 1818. The neighbouring palace, **Palazzo Contarini delle Figure**, from the early 16th century, owes its name to the caryatids holding up the balcony.

Situated on a bend of the canal and bordering the Rio di Ca' Foscari, the **Palazzo Balbi** dates from the Renaissance but has some baroque decoration on the façade. It is the seat of the regional council of Venetia. Opposite, the magnificent Gothic **Ca' Foscari** is home to the University.

Major exhibitions are held in the **Palazzo Grassi**, which is on your left next to the small church of **San Samuele**, whose square tower dates from the 12th century. The **Ca' Rezzonico** opposite is the prestigious address of the Museum of Decorative Arts. This palace remained unfinished for almost a century following the death of the architect Longhena during its construction.

Approaching the **Ponte dell'Accademia**, a wooden bridge with a single span, you will see on your right the **Gallerie dell' Accademia**, the Academy of Fine Arts. Further on, **Ca' Venier dei Leoni**, a somewhat lower building than its neighbours, is in fact an unfinished palace, bought by Peggy Guggenheim to house her collection of modern paintings. It is said that in the 18th century the Venier family kept a lion tied up in the courtyard, hence the name of their palace. The huge **Palazzo Corner**, also known as Ca' Grande, was built by Sansovino in 1537. Today it is the Prefecture of Venice.

Looking once more at the right bank, you see the attractive **Palazzo Dario** (1487) with its Renaissance façade encrusted with polychrome marble. Soon you come upon the superb **Basilica of Santa Maria della Salute**, a masterpiece by Longhena, built in 1630 in gratitude to the Virgin for having brought to an end the epidemic of plague. After the **Dogana da Mar**, the last building on the right bank, the waterway opens into Saint Mark's canal. On the belfry of the customs house *(dogana)* two bronze figures support a golden sphere surmounted by the statue of Fortune.

Finally, you arrive at the Piazza San Marco, and it is time to come back to earth and admire this wonderful living museum.

ITCHY FEET

The bold bronze chargers over the main portal of San Marco once crowned Trajan's Arch in Rome, but no one knows where they first came from. They later graced the imperial hippodrome of Constantinople, until Doge Dandolo took the city and the horses in 1204. In Venice they guarded the Arsenal for a while, then trotted over to San Marco. Napoleon, however, carted them off to Paris where they were harnessed to a chariot in the Tuileries Gardens; the Austrians brought them back. During each of the world wars, the horses were sent outside the city for safe-keeping. The Venetians vowed that their horses would stay put. But a different kind of threat caused a change of plan. The horses were moved inside, safe from the effects of pollution, and replicas now stand on the balcony of the basilica.

❏ *THE DISTRICTS*

SAN MARCO

This is the historic, political, cultural and architectural centre of the city. Here, within the southern loop of the Grand Canal, you find most of the historic monuments and churches, as well as many restaurants, shops, big hotels and banks.

SAN POLO

In the centre of Venice, this is the smallest of the *sestieri,* containing many churches and great schools, as well as the Rialto, one of the first inhabited areas of the city. From the 10th century until the present day it has been a retail centre.

SANTA CROCE

The east part of this district has retained its old palaces that give onto the Grand Canal. On the west side, however, the old dwellings have been replaced by an industrial zone.

DORSODURO

This is the intellectual district, with the University, museums, public and private collections and foundations. In the southern part of Venice, it is a quiet residential area, considered to be one of the most pleasant places in which to live.

CANNAREGIO

This is the true heart of Venice, a *sestiere* of small businesses and workshops, and one of the most populous. It takes up all of the northwest sector of the city between the Grand Canal and the lagoon. In the centre is the Ghetto, a small island surrounded by water where for three centuries all the Jews were forced to live.

29

CASTELLO

This *sestiere* was probably given its name because of a castle erected here in Roman times. It is the most extensive of the districts of Venice, and owes its charm to its working-class atmosphere.

The establishment of the Arsenal in the 12th century was crucial to the development of this part of town. Here is the Rio Terrà Garibaldi, the longest street in Venice, as well as the Salizzada San Lio, an important commercial road which has retained two interesting examples of 13th-century Byzantine tower-houses with a connecting arch.

At the extreme eastern edge of the urban area, the Isola di San Pietro was the first of all the islands in the lagoon to be inhabited, possibly in the late 6th century.

❏ *QUAYS AND WATERWAYS*

RIO DI SAN TROVASO

Dorsoduro

This canal links the Grand Canal and the Giudecca Canal. Patrician palaces line its quays, some going back to the 14th century.

The Palazzo Contarini degli Scrigni is made up of two adjoining buildings with two façades, one Gothic and the other 17th century. Other noteworthy edifices are the Giustinian-Recanati, Nani and Sangiantoffetti palaces.

ZATTERE

Dorsoduro

This long quay runs from the Customs Point as far as San Basegio, bordering the Giudecca Canal for 2 km (over a mile). Used for tying up the rafts *(zattere)* which transported wood brought from the mainland, it was an area of intense activity. Today it is a most pleasant walk, sunny and sheltered from the gusts of the *bora,* offering lovely views of La Giudecca from its terraces.

FONDAMENTA DELLA SENSA

Cannaregio

The long line of the della Sensa Canal and the regular succession of its various urban elements (canal, quay, buildings, gardens), provide surprising perspectives. Its southerly aspect, tranquillity and greenery have encouraged the construction of some handsome palaces.

FONDAMENTA NUOVE

Cannaregio

This quay offers a magnificent view of the vast stretch of water and the nearest islands (San Michele and Murano) of the northern lagoon. But when the north wind *(tramontana)* is blowing, it is a touch too exposed for a comfortable walk!

FONDAMENTA VENIER-SAVORGNAN
Cannaregio

This quay borders the wide and luminous Cannaregio Canal. See the two splendid palaces, Palazzo Priuli-Manfrin, in neoclassical style, and the 17th-century Palazzo Savorgnan, with its luxuriant gardens open to the public.

RIVA DEGLI SCHIAVONI
Castello

Leading from San Marco to the public gardens, this quay is the ideal walk for soaking up the atmosphere of Venice. Long and lively, with souvenir stalls and artists, its name comes from the Schiavonian or Slavonic (Dalmatian) seafarers who conducted their business here. Luxury hotels and palaces, mostly 19th-century, line this quay: the Palazzo delle Prigioni in Istrian stone, the Palazzo Dandolo which is now the prestigious Danieli Hotel, and the Palazzo Gabrielli, also a hotel.

❑ *BRIDGES*

PONTE DEI SOSPIRI
San Marco

This is the infamous bridge which leads from the Palazzo Ducale to the prisons. Built in the 17th century in the baroque style, it has two parallel corridors used to take prisoners to their cells (the *piombi*, under the roof, and the *pozzi*, in the cellars). As they passed the windows of the bridge, the hapless captives could see the lagoon, perhaps for the last time… hence "The Bridge of Sighs".

PONTE DELL'ACCADEMIA
San Marco

Erected across the Grand Canal in 1934 to replace an earlier iron bridge, this wooden structure was originally intended to be temporary: it has recently been reinforced with steel. Offering a wonderful view of the Customs Point, it leads into the *sestiere* of Dorsoduro.

PONTE DI RIALTO
San Marco

The imposing white marble arch of the Rialto Bridge spans the Grand Canal at its narrowest point. First a floating bridge of boats, then built of wood, it collapsed several times before 1500. After considering plans by Michelangelo, Sansovino and others, the Republic awarded the reconstruction work to Antonio Da Ponte.

PONTE DELLE TETTE
San Polo

In the part of town known as *delle Carampane,* the "Nipples Bridge" was somewhat disreputable. When

31

they crossed over, prospective clients could see the prostitutes displaying their charms from the windows of the houses opposite. This entire zone was given over to brothels, encouraged by the Venetian authorities who hoped thereby to contain the widespread practice of homosexuality.

PONTE DEGLI SCALZI
Santa Croce
The most recent of the Grand Canal's bridges was renovated in 1934 by Eugenio Miozzi, replacing an iron structure built by the Austrians in 1858.

PONTE DEI PUGNI
Dorsoduro
Along the Fondamenta Gherardini, a large boat stacked with vegetables is tied up under the bridge—a picturesque floating shop. Above it, the Ponte dei Pugni (The Bridge of Fists) is so called because there are four imprints in the marble to show the place where adversaries in fist-fights used to stand in days of yore.

PONTE DELLE GUGLIE
Cannaregio
Built in a single span in 1580, this bridge has four obelisks on its balustrade. It leads to the fish and vegetable market held on Rio Terrà San Leonardo.

❏ SQUARES AND GARDENS
A few charming corners where you can escape the crowds—or the sun.

CAMPO SAN GIACOMO DELL'ORIO
Santa Croce
The shady trees in this rare green haven in the town centre make a pleasant summer setting for shows and festivals.

GIARDINO PAPADOPOLI
Santa Croce
This very large garden was already famous at the beginning of the century for the profusion and quality of its plants. It was created in about 1810 on the site of several houses and the church and monastery of Santa Croce. To reach it, cross over the Ponte dei Tolentini.

CAMPO DELLA MOSCA
Dorsoduro
This square owes its name to the many workshops which used to produce "flies", the black taffeta beauty spots which ladies used to stick on their face to emphasize the whiteness of their skin (or to hide their spots).

CAMPO SANTA MARGHERITA
Dorsoduro
The centre of social life of the *sestiere*, this tree-lined *campo* has

CARNIVAL

From the early Middle Ages until the end of the 18th century, Venetians took full advantage of the period of freedom which was accorded them between December 26 and Shrove Tuesday, before the privations of Lent. People of all social strata came from every corner of Europe to enjoy themselves and, hidden behind a mask, to play all kinds of pranks. It was spoilsport Napoleon who put an end to these amusements. At the end of the 1970s, the Mayor of Venice had the idea of reviving the Carnival, which has subsequently become an unrivalled festival with parades, theatre, opera and other events, where the made-up and masked spectators are often the best part of the show.

always been used as a market place. The houses which line it are rather modest, except for a few palaces which still recall the Byzantine or Gothic styles. Next to the derelict church is a campanile with a marble baroque dragon at the base.

CAMPO DELLA MADDALENA
Cannaregio
Quiet and off the beaten track, this *campo* is particularly beautiful, characterized by its simple houses topped with imposing chimneys.

CORTE DEL MILION
Cannaregio
The area which stretches behind the church of San Giovanni Crisostomo is called the Corte del Milion. Tradition has it that Marco Polo lived here in No. 5845 until his death in 1324. Several buildings present architectural elements from different eras: observe the Byzantine friezes on the walls.

CAMPO DELLE GORNE
Castello
A quiet area, bordered on one side by the canal of the same name. Beyond the canal rises the high wall of the Arsenal, decorated with great stone gargoyles *(gorne)* which overlook the low buildings of this working-class area, creating eerie effects.

GIARDINI PUBBLICI
Castello
On the Riva dei Sette Martiri, this is the only green space of truly urban dimensions. Napoleon had these gardens made on marshland, but the original neoclassical design was modified with the introduction of the Biennale Internazionale d'Arte (see p. 25). Many 18th-century statues stand among the greenery. The *Monument to a Partisan,* in the waters of the lagoon, is without doubt the most poignant.

Shopping

Venice is a shopper's paradise, where you can find anything from a straw hat to hand-made glassware from Murano. Prices are quite steep, but this is Venice, after all. Shops are generally open from 9 a.m. until 12.30 and from 3 p.m. until 7.30 p.m. In summer, they stay open during the lunch hour and on Sundays.

❏ SHOPPING STREETS

The most exclusive shops cluster around Piazza San Marco, while the main shopping street, the Merceria, is lined with appealing boutiques with more competitive prices. Budget-priced goods beckon around the Rialto and on Strada Nuovo leading to the railway station.

❏ CRAFTS

Costume jewellery abounds in Venice at reasonable prices. Gold and silver pieces, including some marvellous filigree, are fairly expensive but show the stamp of Venetian craftsmanship. Leather goods and silk are definitely worth considering. If you want something truly typical of Venice, look for 17th- or 18th-century theatrical and carnival masks of papier-mâché; gondolier slippers, normally made of velvet with rope soles, or a gondolier's straw hat with coloured band. The women of Burano make exquisite lace. The Murano glassware you see everywhere is not up to the old standards, but if you have a discerning eye you might find something attractive.

CODOGNATO
Calle Seconda a l'Ascension 1295, San Marco
Well-known for heavy, richly decorated jewellery, antique and modern. October–March the shop is closed on Monday mornings.

FURLA
Mercerie del Capitello 4954, San Marco
A world of leather objects of all shapes; very original.

JESURUM
Piazza San Marco 60–61
This celebrated store has been supplying lace work for more than a hundred years.

«M» OGGETTI D'ARTE
Frezzeria 1691, San Marco
Art nouveau jewellery, clothing and furnishing fabrics printed in antique style.

MISSIAGLIA
Piazza San Marco 125
A Venetian institution for almost 150 years. Handmade objets d'art in gold and precious stones.

NARDI
Piazza San Marco 68–72
Under the sign of the Moors, brooches and rings, bracelets and necklaces.

PAULY & C.
Ponte Consorzi Calle Longa 4391/A, San Marco
Inside the palace, a sophisticated collection of hats, glasses, furniture and marble objects. The second shop in Piazza San Marco sells Murano glassware, vases, light-fittings and lampshades.

VALESE
Calle Fiubera 793, San Marco
Very fashionable, the Venetian masks sold here are in brass.

VENEZIARTIGIANA
Calle Larga 412/3 San Marco
A cooperative for Venetian craftsmen making objects in glass or

paper, costume jewellery, as well as masks.

VENINI
Piazzetta dei Leoncini 314,
San Marco
Renowned throughout the world for glassware and designer objects. There is a second shop on Murano.

ZANCOPE
Calle de le Ostreghe 2360,
San Marco
Delicate glassware of exquisite workmanship.

BAMBOLANDIA
Ponte della Madoneta 1462,
San Polo
Restoration and reproduction of antique dolls.

CENERENTOLA
Calle dei Saoneri 2721,
San Polo
A festival of antique handmade lace.

CICOGNA
Campo San Tomà 2867,
San Polo
A "historic" family of restorers and gilders of wood.

LA SCIALUPPA
Calle seconda dei Saoneri 2681,
San Polo
Scale models of all kinds of ships.

MONDONOVO MASCHERE
Rio terrà Canal 3063,
Dorsoduro
Handsome masks for the carnival, the theatre and cinema.

SIGNOR BLUM
Campo San Barnaba 2840,
Dorsoduro
Everything in wood: scenes of Venice, miniature palace façades, trinkets and games of patience.

TOTEM – IL CANALE
Ponte dell'Accademia 878/B,
Dorsoduro
African jewellery and small exhibitions featuring young artists.

FUSETTI & DIEGO
Calle Ghetto Vecchio 1219,
Cannaregio
A shop specializing in Jewish crafts. Handsome objects in silver filigree and glass chalices from Murano.

RIZZI PAOLO
Sottoportego Bragadin 2258,
Cannaregio
Near Strada Nova, one of the best artisan goldsmiths in town. He makes embossed engravings.

VENTURINI
Sottoportego delle Colonnette 2147–49,
Cannaregio

A workshop producing limited series of violas, violins, cellos and double-basses.

BAROVIER & DONÀ
Fondamenta San Lorenzo,
Murano
A dynasty of glassblowers, established in 1324.

CARLO MORETTI
Fondamenta Manin 23,
Murano
Principally glasses and furnishing accessories of modern design.

ERCOLE MORETTI
Fondamenta Navagero 42,
Murano
The finest *murrine* (glass jewellery), beads and buttons to be found on the island.

SEGUSO VETRI D'ARTE
Ponte Vivarini 138,
Murano
Antique models in modern sandy glass.

❏ BOOKS AND PICTURES

BOHM
Salizzada San Moisè 1349/50,
San Marco
18th- and 19th-century prints and modern lithographs.

FANTONI
Salizzada San Luca 4121,
San Marco
The most complete art bookshop in the historic centre of Venice.

IL PAPIRO
Calle del Piovan 2764,
San Marco
Overflowing with writing materials; paper, pens, inks and notebooks.

LIBRERIA ANTIQUARIA
Viale XXII Marzo 2424,
San Marco
Old books and many Venetian prints.

GRAFFITI
Campo dei Frari,
Salizzada San Rocco 3045,
San Polo
A small shop selling posters, postcards and reproductions of pictures by great artists.

LIBRERIA TOLETTA
Calle della Toletta 1214,
Dorsoduro
Reduced price books, dictionaries in every language, art books and critical works.

NORELENE
Campo San Vio,
Calle della Chiesa 727,
Dorsoduro

37

Wonderful prints, produced by hand on silk, velours and crêpe de Chine.

LIBRERIA SOLARIS
Rio Terrà 2332,
Cannaregio
Specializes in strip cartoons and science fiction.

LIBRERIA FILIPPI
Calle del Paradiso 5763,
Castello
The best publications about Venice, its history and art, as well as small collections of fables by Venetian authors.

SANTI GIOVANNI E PAOLO
Calle Santi Giovanni e Paolo
6358/A, Castello
All the latest in "alternative" books. They can obtain any book you want within a few days, especially foreign works in the original language.

❏ FASHION

AL DUCA D'AOSTA
San Marco 4945/46
Even the most difficult of men can find everything here, from underpants to overcoats.

ARABA FENICE
Calle dei Barcaroli 1821,
San Marco

An imaginative designer who uses only natural fabrics.

BOTTEGA VENETA
Calle Vallaresso 1337,
San Marco
Accessories in all colours of leather and suede. Excellent quality.

FRANZ
Calle del Spezier 2770/A,
San Marco
Silk clothing and lingerie. Franz Baby, Calle San Luca 4578/A, is the Franz shop for children, elegant clothing in vaguely retro style.

BALOCOLOC
Calle del Scaleter 2235,
San Polo
Hats for every taste, from the Venetian tricorn to the gondolier's boater. All handmade.

VOLPE
Calle di Mezzo 1228,
San Polo
Clothes by the great fashion designers. Everything for the elegant gentleman.

AMINA MI
Campiello Flaminio Corner 5601,
Cannaregio
Using fabrics by the great designers, the workshop of this small shop produces greatly sought-after

clothing in the latest styles. Go prepared to seize an opportunity.

CACAO
Cannaregio 5583/86
An unusual shop for youngsters who want to be smart but trendy.

COIN
Salizzada San Giovanni Crisostomo 5790, Cannaregio
The biggest shoe-shop in Venice, housed in a 15th-century palace.

MARINELLO CALZATURE SPORT
Calle del Pistor 1902, Cannaregio
Sports shoes of every kind and every make.

LA CORTE DELLE FATE
Salizzada San Lio 5690, Castello
If you want a pair of the most extravagant shoes imaginable as your souvenir of Venice, then visit this unbelievable shop.

❏ MARKETS
Venice flourished as a commercial city through trade with the Orient. Cargoes of exotic goods were unloaded at the markets near the Rialto and by the Grand Canal. Even today, these markets are very busy.

ERBERIA
Rialto
Open in the morning. A fruit and vegetable market with some stalls selling clothing and souvenirs.

MERCATINO ANTIQUARIATO
Campo San Maurizio, San Marco Christmas, Easter and during the Regata Storica
Attractive antiques market, worth looking at closely.

PESCHERIA
Campo della Pescheria, Rialto
A covered fish market, held in the morning. A sight not to be missed.

RIALTO
Campo delle Beccarie
A bustling and picturesque morning market.

RIO TERRÀ SAN LEONARDO
Ponte delle Guglie, Cannaregio
A picturesque fruit and vegetable market held daily.

RIO TERRÀ GARIBALDI
Castello
The centre of a working class quarter, always enlivened by this busy market.

SANTA MARIA FORMOSA
Campo Santa Maria Formosa, Castello
A food and clothing market.

Dining Out

This section describes medium-priced restaurants, where you can eat well at a reasonable cost, in the range of 40,000 to 60,000 lire. If you want a snack or a less formal atmosphere, see under "Bacari". Venice boasts some excellent local dishes but is best renowed for the superb seafood. For most of the year you can eat outdoors, enjoying the passing parade as much as your meal.

❏ RESTAURANTS

AI MERCANTI
Corte Coppo 4346/A,
San Marco
Tel. 523 82 69. Closed Sunday
and Monday morning.
Excellent fish dishes.

ARTURO
Calle degli Assassini 3656/A,
San Marco
Tel. 528 69 74. Closed Sunday.
Meat specialities, fresh produce (good *misto di verdure*). Venetian clientele. Reservation essential; credit cards not accepted.

CONTE PESCAOR
Piscina San Zulian 597/A,
San Marco
Tel. 522 14 83. Closed Sunday.
Wonderful fish dishes to be enjoyed
in a typical Venetian atmosphere.

DA RAFFAELE
Fondamenta delle Ostreghe 2347,
San Marco
Tel. 528 99 40. Closed Thursday.
Fish a speciality, fresh and
well-prepared.

ANTICA TRATTORIA POSTE VECIE
Pescheria 1608,
San Polo
Tel. 721 822. Closed Tuesday.
A very good restaurant with a
pleasant terrace (in season) shaded
by a pergola. Delicious fish *risotti*.

ANTICA BESSETA
Salizzada de Ca' Zusto 1395,
Santa Croce
Tel. 721 687. Closed Tuesday and
Wednesday.
A very well-known and
well-frequented small restaurant.
The traditional Venetian *risotti* are
truly excellent, as are all the fish
specialities. It's best to reserve.

LA ZUCCA
Ramo del Megio 1762,
Santa Croce
Tel. 524 15 70. Closed Sunday.

A wide choice of vegetarian dishes,
but also soups, meat dishes and
couscous.

LA FURATOLA
Calle Longa San Barnaba 2870/A,
Dorsoduro
Tel. 520 85 94. Closed Thursday.
An old-established restaurant
serving very high quality dishes.

LOCANDA MONTIN
Fondamenta di Borgo 1147,
Dorsoduro
Tel. 522 71 51. Closed Tuesday
evening and Wednesday.
The favourite restaurant of the
artistic community. Venetian
cuisine.

A LA VECIA CAVANA
Rio Terà Franceschi 4624/A,
Cannaregio
Tel. 523 86 44. Closed Thursday.
A well-known restaurant close to
Campo Santi Apostoli. Specializes in
fish dishes.

ALLA PALAZZINA
Rio terrà San Leonardo 1509,
Cannaregio
Tel. 717 725.
Closed Wednesday.
Formely a *bacaro*, this establishment
has been onverted into an elegant
trattoria with a pergola on the Ponte
delle Guglie.

AL VAGON

Sottoportego del Magazen 5597, Cannaregio
Tel. 528 56 26. Closed Tuesday.
Excellent fish to be enjoyed on a charming terrace.

ANTICA MOLA

Fondamenta degli Ormesini 2800, Cannaregio
Tel. 717 492.
A good trattoria in the Ghetto neighbourhood, patronized principally by Venetians. Garden and waterside terrace.

IL PARADISO PERDUTO

Fondamenta della Misericordia 2540, Cannaregio
Tel. 720 581. Closed Wednesday.
A stylish bistro serving traditional food to the accompaniment of good music.

AL GIARDINETTO

Salizzada Zorzi 4928, Castello
Tel. 528 53 32. Closed Thursday.
In the Palazzo Zorzi, which dates from 1400, this is a typical trattoria with pergola where you can eat outside in fine weather.

CORTE SCONTA

Calle del Pestrin 3886, Castello
Tel. 522 70 24. Closed Sunday and Monday.
An old bistrot renovated with taste but keeping its traditional atmosphere. The high quality cooking (fish only) is a match for the most sophisticated restaurants. Reservation advisable.

HOSTARIA DA FRANZ

Fondamenta San Isepo 754, Castello
Tel. 522 08 61. Closed Tuesday.
Exceptional seafood spaghetti and for dessert, a *tiramisù* to die for. During the week open for dinner only, but on Saturday and Sunday lunch is also served.

NUOVA RIVETTA

Ponte di San Provolo 4625, Castello
Tel. 528 73 02. Closed Monday.
An unpretentious bistrot, always full. Try the Venetian-style liver and the cuttlefish cooked in their ink.

ALTANELLA

Calle delle Erbe 268, La Giudecca
Tel. 522 77 80. Closed Monday and Tuesday.
A typical trattoria with service on the terrace in summer. A classical Venetian menu.

HARRY'S DOLCI

Fondamenta San Biagio 773, La Giudecca
Tel. 522 48 44. Closed Tuesday.

Salads and cold food and dazzling desserts—luxury at everyday prices. In summer, sit on the terrace with a view of the San Marco Canal.

ALL'ARTIGLIERE
Via Sandro Gallo 83, Lido
Tel. 526 54 80. Closed Tuesday.
Friendly welcome; excellent traditional cuisine. Try the *spaghetti all'artigliera* (with shellfish).

DA CICIO
Via Sandro Gallo 241, Lido
Tel. 526 06 49. Closed Tuesday.
Famous for its fish *alla griglia.*

AI FRATI
Fondamenta Venier 4,
Murano
Tel. 736 694. Closed Thursday.
Fish a speciality and excellent home-made cakes.

AL GATTO NERO
Fondamenta Giudecca 88,
Burano
Tel. 730 120. Closed Monday.
Delicious *risotto alla buranella* and *pasticcio di pesce.*

LOCANDA CIPRIANI
Piazza Santa Fosca 29, Torcello
Tel. 730 150. Closed Tuesday and all winter.
Sophisticated cooking and rather expensive.

❏ *BACARI*
To munch a *cicheto,* the traditional Venetian snack, while sipping an *ombra* (a glass) of wine, you must call in at one of these old bistros known as *bacari,* perhaps in honour of Bacchus, or of the *bacara,* a wine-jug in the local dialect. People tend to congregate here just before lunch or dinner, to meet up with friends and sample savoury dishes like meatballs, hard-boiled eggs, sandwiches, fried fish, garlic bread, smoked ham, and so on. It's the usual custom to eat standing up in the *bacari,* although some do have a few tables.

The Veneto area produces a number of pleasant red and white wines. The best local reds are Valpolicella, Valpantena and Bardolino—all light and dry; Soave is the most famous white from the region. From Friuli come Pinot Grigio and Pinot Bianco, two dry whites.

AI ASSASSINI
Rio terrà dei Assassini 3695,
San Marco
Tel. 528 79 86. Closed Sunday.
Excellent salads and grilled meats accompanied by good wines. Reservation advisable.

AL VOLTO
Calle Cavalli 4081, San Marco
Tel. 522 89 45. Closed Sunday.

43

Five hundred wines to choose from and a simple but delicious menu.

LE CHAT QUI RIT
Calle Tron 1131,San Marco
Tel. 522 90 86. Closed Saturday.
Self-service with typical dishes such as fried fish and *frittura mista*.

OSTERIA ALLE BOTTEGHE
Calle delle Botteghe 3454,
San Marco
Tel. 522 81 81. Closed Sunday.
Toast with cheese, and *porchetta* (roast suckling pig) sandwiches.

PICCOLO MARTINI
Frezzaria 1501, San Marco
Tel. 528 51 36.
An establishment which recalls the cafés of the turn of the century. The spaghetti *al ragù* (meat and tomato sauce) is unequalled.

ROSTICCERIA SAN BARTOLOMEO
San Marco 5423
Tel. 522 35 69. Closed Monday.
This is the place to try Venetian style *baccalà* (dried cod).

SAN VIDAL
Campo San Stefano 2862/A,
San Marco
Tel. 528 78 43. Closed Wednesday.
Frequented by students who appreciate the hot sandwiches with peppers and aubergines.

AGLI AMICI
Calle Botteri 1544, San Polo
Tel. 524 13 09. Closed Wednesday.
A pleasant trattoria where you'll soon feel at home.

ANTICO DOLO
Ruga Vecchia San Giovanni 778,
Calle del Fighèr 798, San Polo
Tel. 522 65 46. Closed Sunday.
This venerable Venetian establishment offers a wide choice of excellent pasta and rice dishes as well as an exceptional *baccalà*.

CANTINA DO MORI
Calle do Mori 429, San Polo
Tel. 522 54 01.
Closed Wednesday afternoon
and Sunday.
One of the oldest and most famous *bacari* in town, said to go back to the 15th century. There is an incredible choice of wines, and a variety of *cicheti* to be sampled while you stand.

CANTINA DO SPADE
Sottoportego do Spade 860,
San Polo
Tel. 521 05 74. Closed Sunday
and Thursday lunch.
Established in 1475: Casanova himself came here. You may sit down (if you can find an empty seat) to try the pasta and rice dishes, fish sandwiches and game *cicheti*.

VINI DA PINTO
Campo delle Beccarie 367,
San Polo
Tel. 522 45 99. Closed Sunday
evening and Monday.
This has been the ultimate *bacaro*
for about a century. Cooked
sausages, *baccalà* (salt cod) and
good wines.

DA CODROMA
Ponte del Soccorso 2540,
Dorsoduro
Tel. 524 67 89. Closed Thursday.
Good wine and *cicheti* until 1 a.m.,
frequently to the accompaniment of
jazz (Friday, rhythm and blues).

VINI AL BOTTEGON
Fondamenta Nani 992,
Dorsoduro
Tel. 523 00 24. Closed Sunday.
A wide choice of wines and
sandwiches.

AL MILION
Corte del Milion 5841, Cannaregio
Tel. 522 93 02. Closed Wednesday.
Venetian dishes, such as liver and
cuttlefish, in what was once the
house of Marco Polo.

ALLA BOMBA
Calle dell'Oca 4297, Cannaregio
Tel. 523 74 52. Closed Wednesday.
An unpretentious *bacaro*, but very
popular. Seafood specialities.

ALLA MADDALENA
Rio terrà della Maddalena 2348,
Cannaregio
Tel. 720 723. Closed Sunday.
Traditional sandwiches are served
here, but best of all is the *pasta e
fasoi* (pasta with beans).

ARDENGHI
Calle della Testa 6369,
Cannaregio
Tel. 523 76 91. Open 6 p.m. to
midnight. Closed Sunday.
An eclectic bistro with the bonus of
good music. Typical Venetian
cuisine. Reservation essential.

CA' D'ORO
Ramo Ca' d'Oro 3912,
Cannaregio
Tel. 528 53 24. Closed Thursday.
A luxurious and well-restored
bacaro, where you would be well
advised to try the delicious fried
vegetables *(misto di verdure)* or, in
the evening, the starters.

TIZIANO SNACK BAR
Salizzada San Giovanni
Cristostomo 5747,
Cannaregio
Tel. 523 55 44.
The only pizzeria in town which
sells pizza by the metre. This
establishment is also a favourite of
devotees of *pasta al forno*
(oven-baked pasta dishes).

ALLE TESTIERE

Calle del Mondo Novo 5801,
Castello
Tel. 522 72 20. Closed Sunday.
Traditional dishes together with a few original culinary creations. Fish specialities.

TRATTORIA DA BRUNO

Salizzada San Lio,
Calle del Paradiso 5731,
Castello
Tel. 522 14 80. Closed Tuesday.
A wide choice of fish and seafood, meat and game. Two minutes from Piazza San Marco.

AI CACCIATORI

Fondamenta dei Vetrai,
Murano
Closed Sunday.
The only genuine *bacaro* on the island.

❏ *CAFÉS, ICE-CREAM PARLOURS AND TEAROOMS*

Light meals, pastries and other desserts, and all types of drinks are served in the cafés. Prices vary from place to place, and depend on whether you are at the bar, at an inside table, or on the terrace.
If you find Italian espresso too strong for your taste, ask for a *caffè lungo* (with extra water) or a *cappuccino* with milk.

CAFFÈ FLORIAN

Piazza San Marco 56/59
Tel. 528 53 38.
Closed Wednesday.
Famous throughout Europe since 1720, this is one of the symbols of Venice. A meeting place for intellectuals, it is enjoying a revival. The coffee is always fantastic.

GRAN CAFFÈ QUADRI

Piazza San Marco 120
Tel. 522 21 05. Closed Monday.
A 19th-century establishment with a small restaurant, historically a rival to Florian. Both claim to have introduced Turkish coffee to Venice.

PASTICCERIA DAL COL

Calle dei Fabbri 1035, San Marco
Tel. 520 55 29.
Closed Sunday.
Delicious home-made cakes, all cream, and *zabaglione*.

PASTICCERIA ROSA SALVA

Campo San Luca 4589, San Marco
Tel. 522 53 85. Closed Sunday.
A dynasty of pastrycooks—a true institution. (Other branches: Calle Fiubera 951, tel. 521 05 44; Mercerie San Salvador 5020, tel. 522 79 34).

BAR GELATERIA AL CUCCIOLO

Fondamenta Zattere ai Gesuiti
782, Dorsoduro
Tel. 528 96 41. Closed Monday.

Well-known to greedy Venetians, who cannot resist a hazelnut or coffee ice while strolling along the Zattere.

IL CAFFÈ
Campo Santa Margherita 2963, Dorsoduro
Tel. 528 79 98. Closed Sunday.
An establishment with a nostalgic air, at the heart of the *sestiere*.

DA NICO
Fondamenta Zattere ai Gesuiti 922, Dorsoduro
Tel. 522 52 93. Closed Thursday.
The best ice-cream in town—veritable masterpieces.

PASTICCERIA F.LLI COLUSSI
Dorsoduro 2867
Tel. 523 18 71. Closed Tuesday.
Typical cakes made to traditional Venetian recipes, and wonderful homemade jams.

CAFFÈ CAUSIN DA RENATO
Campo Santa Margherita 2996, Dorsoduro
Tel. 523 60 91. Closed Saturday.
An absolute must for lovers of delectable nougat ice-cream

PASTICCERIA VIO
Calle seconda de la Toletta 1192, Dorsoduro
Tel. 522 74 51. Closed Thursday.

A good idea for an edible souvenir: Venetian marzipan cakes.

PASTICCERIA ZANON MARIO
Fondamenta della Toletta 1169/A, Dorsoduro
Tel. 522 26 19. Closed Wednesday.
This tearoom is extremely popular with students from the nearby Academy of Fine Arts. No doubt they find inspiration in the meringues and apple doughnuts.

DAL MAS
Lista di Spagna 150/A, Cannaregio
Closed Tuesday.
For a great start to your day, come here for a standing breakfast. You will never forget it!

FUGASSA
Calle de l'Anconetta 1979, Cannaregio
Closed Tuesday.
The house specialities are a kind of bread called *foccacie alla venexana* and the now world-famous *semifreddi: tiramisù al mascarpone*.

DIDOVICH
Campo Santa Marina 5909, Castello
Tel. 523 00 17. Closed Sunday.
An extraordinary tearoom, where everything is homemade.

Entertainment

Although there are countless things to do during the day, Venice has little to offer the night-owl by way of entertainment. As darkness falls, the city settles down to sleep; even in summer it is difficult to find anything open after midnight. The principal nocturnal pastime is a stroll through the deserted streets. If you fancy something more exciting, try one of the following.

❏ *BARS AND PIANO BARS*

AL TEATRO
Campo San Fantin 1916, San Marco
Open daily (except Monday, off-season) 7.30 a.m.–2 a.m.

A very popular bar with a pleasant terrace.

FLORIAN
Piazza San Marco
Open daily (except Tuesday) 7.30 a.m.–midnight.

The most typical Venetian bar, very select. To the strains of the orchestra in its 18th-century rooms, one can enjoy a drink, a cup of tea or a little something to eat.

HAIG'S BAR

Campo Santa Maria del Giglio 2477, San Marco
Open daily (except Wednesday) 10 a.m.–2 a.m.
This is the ideal place for night-owls, quiet and not too expensive.

HARRY'S BAR

Calle Vallaresso 1323, San Marco
Open daily 10.30 a.m.–11 p.m.
Soak up the atmosphere while sipping a "Bellini" in this bar, once the haunt of Hemingway and now a favourite of actors, writers and politicians. Very expensive, but just for once…

IL CHERUBINO

Campo San Luca, San Marco
Open daily (except Monday) 9 a.m.–3 a.m.
A small establishment frequented by young people, intellectuals and insomniacs.

MARTINI SCALA CLUB

Campiello San Gaetano 1980, San Marco
Open every evening (except Tuesday) 10 p.m.–3-30 a.m.
Close to the La Fenice theatre, this select piano-bar is both a "Live Music Bar" and a "Night Restaurant".

AI POSTALI

Fondamenta Rio Marin 821, Santa Croce
Open every evening (except Tuesday) 6 p.m.–2 a.m.
A small bar with a youngish clientèle.

CORNER PUB

Calle della Chiesa 684, Dorsoduro
Open daily (except Tuesday) 10 a.m.–11 p.m.
A small pub, well-known to the English and English-speakers in general.

LINEA D'OMBRA

Fondamenta delle Zattere ai Saloni 19, Ponte dell'Umilità, Dorsoduro
Open every evening (except Wednesday and Sunday) 7 p.m.–2 a.m.
A small place where one can eat or just enjoy a drink while listening to jazz.

IL PARADISO PERDUTO

Fondamenta della Misericordia 2540, Cannaregio

*Open every evening (except
Wednesday) 6.30 p.m.–1 a.m.*
A restaurant-bar where jazz is
played and where songwriters and
composers try out their latest works
(see also p. 42)

DO LEONI

*Riva degli Schiavoni 4176,
Castello*
A piano bar for discriminating
people.

❏ DISCOTHEQUES

CLUB EL SOUK

*Calle Corfu 1056/A,
Dorsoduro
Open 10 p.m.–4 a.m.*
A small place and always crowded.
Bar open from 10 a.m. to 6–10 p.m.
Booking compulsory.

ACROPOLIS

*Lungomare Marconi 22, Lido
Open daily in summer;
from end September to May,
Saturday evening only.*
A pleasant disco which overlooks
the Lido beach.

❏ CASINO

The municipal Casino of Venice is at
Lungomare Marconi 4, Lido, during
the summer and at Palazzo

Vendramin-Calergi, Cannaregio, in
winter. The Casino is open
every evening, and evening dress
is required.
If you don't want to tempt Fate at
the gambling tables, you can just
have a drink and listen to the music
in the nightclub.

❏ THEATRES
AND CONCERT HALLS

SALA CONCERTI DEL CIRCOLO ARTISTICO

*Palazzo delle Prigioni,
San Marco
Tel. 522 57 07.*

TEATRO DEL RIDOTTO

*Calle Vallaresso 1332,
San Marco
Tel. 522 29 39.*

TEATRO GOLDONI

*Calle del Teatro o de la Comedia
4650/B, San Marco
Tel. 520 54 22.*

PALAFENICE

*Tronchetto, opposite Stazione
Marittima
Vaporetto line 82*
A tented opera house to replace
La Fenice until restoration is
completed. Nothing can stop the
Venice Opera season!

The Islands

The Venice lagoon is a small inland sea more than 50 km (30 miles) long and 8–14 km (5–9 miles) wide, with a surface area of over 550 sq km (215 sq miles). To become acquainted with the islands is to understand more of Venice and a unique world. Of the inhabited islands, the biggest are La Giudecca, San Giorgio Maggiore, Lido, Murano, Burano and Torcello.

❏ LA GIUDECCA

Two minutes from the Zattere by vaporetto line 82.

Three quays—Fondamenta della Croce, delle Zitelle and di San Giovanni—lie alongside the Canale della Giudecca. At the western end there are several small 15th-century palaces and an unusual Gothic structure called the Stucky Windmill, built in 1896 by a Swiss industrialist.

IL REDENTORE

Fondamenta San Giacomo

In July the *Redentore* procession

ends at this church which is linked to the della Salute church by a bridge of boats. The festival is in memory of a vow made in 1576 when the plague was ravaging the city. Begun by Palladio in 1577 and completed by Antonio da Ponte in 1592, the church contains some fine canvases by Tintoretto, Palma the Younger and Veronese.

SANT'EUFEMIA

Fondamenta Sant'Eufemia.
Built in the 9th century, this church has retained the simple lines of the alterations carried out 200 years later. Within, the three aisles in Venetian-Byzantine style harmonize with the sumptuously decorated walls and ceilings going back to the 18th century.

❏ SAN GIORGIO MAGGIORE

This island is reached by taking the vaporetto from the Zitelle landing-stage on La Giudecca (line 82). It has a large group of Benedictine monastic buildings. The church is dedicated to San Giorgio: it is a masterpiece by Palladio, begun in 1566 but completed after his death. In the interior there are paintings by Ricci, Tintoretto and Carpaccio. The monastery is of great architectural value, as are Palladio's cloister and the refectory.

❏ LIDO

Direct service by vaporetto line 6 from the Riva degli Schiavoni (6 minute crossing).
Lines 1 (frequent stops, journey time about one hour), 52 and 82 (the latter only in summer) also call at the Lido.
If you are in a car, ferry 17 (automezzi) from Tronchetto (crossing time 35 minutes).

Even though the charms of this cosmopolitan seaside resort are a little faded, it is still pleasant to saunter along the promenade by the sea (Lungomare Guglielmo Marconi) and admire the famous Grand Hotel des Bains (which featured in the film *Death in Venice*), the casino, the Mostra del Cinema palace and the Grand Hotel Excelsior. The long beach and the dunes at Alberoni, a small resort at the end of the shore, are worth the walk. Equally typical is the small island of Pellestrina, with its fishing villages and its *murazzi,* sturdy sea-walls to contain the fury of the waves. In the south of the island is the small Malamocco quarter, which grew from the 14th century. There you can see the Palazzo del Podestà and the Santa Maria Assunta church.
It is pleasant to explore the Lido by bicycle: bicycles and tandems may be hired at the intersection of Gran Viale and Via Zara.

SAN NICOLÒ DI LIDO

Benedictine church and monastery founded in the first half of the 11th century, in the northeast corner of the island. It was in this church that Mass was celebrated after the ceremony of the wedding of Venice to the sea. Every year for 800 years, until the abolition of the Republic by Napoleon, the Doge of Venice set out from the Lido towards the open sea on board the magnificent galley Bucintoro, followed by the gondolas of the other leading citizens. There he threw a ring into the waters, saying "We wed ourselves to you, our sea, as a sign of true and perpetual domination". This splendid ceremony has now been revived, but as a tourist attraction.

ANTICO CIMITERO ISRAELITICO

The ancient Jewish cemetery which lies along San Nicolò is one of the oldest in Europe, consecrated in 1389. Tombs and funerary steles from the 14th to the 17th century can be seen.

SAN LAZZARO DEGLI ARMENI

This small island is 500 m (550 yd) from the Lido. It became the home of the Mechitar Fathers of the Roman Catholic Armenian Church in 1717. The monastery is surrounded by a lovely garden and houses a library and a museum which contains paintings, archaeological finds, relics and a precious collection of more than 2,000 Armenian manuscripts).

❏ *MURANO*

Vaporetti lines 52, 12 and 13. Direct service during the tourist season from Fond. Nuove (crossing time 7 minutes).

The quality is not as high as in days gone by, but Murano is still celebrated for its glassware, and remains a separate little world.

BASILICA DEI SANTI MARIA E DONATO

Fondamenta Giustinian

Founded in the 7th century a rebuilt in the 12th century bell-tower, this church is best examples of Venet Byzantine architecture extraordinary, a com depicting animals.

SAN PIETRO MARTIRE

Fondamenta da Mula

Rebuilt between the 15th and 16th centuries, this church houses works by Bellini and Veronese.

MUSEO VETRARIO

Fondamenta Giustinian 8
Open daily (except Wednesday)
10 a.m.–4 p.m.

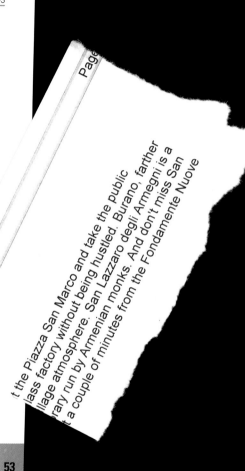

Page
t the Piazza San Marco and take the public
lass factory without being hustled. Burano, farther
llage atmosphere. San Lazzaro degli Armegni is a
rary run by Armenian monks. And don't miss San
t a couple of minutes from the Fondamente Nuove

Situated in the Palazzo Giustinian, this museum contains a collection of superb glassware from the 2nd century BC to the 2nd century AD and from the 15th century to the present.

❏ BURANO

Vaporetto line 12 from Fondamente Nuove (crossing time about 40 minutes).

Fishing was at one time the principal activity of the Buranelli (the inhabitants of Burano), who formed an authentic working community. The women are accomplished lacemakers. The quays *(fondamenta)* Cavanelle, Cao and della Pescheria enclose a picturesque quarter.

SAN MARTINO

Piazza Baldassarre Galuppi

A church built in the 16th century when the parish was founded, flanked by a bell-tower of the 17th century. Inside you can see an exceptional *Crucifixion* by Tiepolo.

MUSEO DEL MERLETTO

San Martino Destro 184
Open daily (except Monday)
9 a.m.–6 p.m.; Sundays and public holidays 10 a.m.–4 p.m.

This museum traces the history of lacemaking which developed in the island at the beginning of the 16th

century. A school and a workshop, still in operation, are adjacent.

❏ TORCELLO

Vaporetto line 12 from Fondamente Nuove (crossing time about 45 minutes).

Of the large settlement established between the 5th and the 10th centuries, nothing remains but the historic centre which is reached by way of the road bordering the Torcello Canal. You arrive at a grassy esplanade surrounded by buildings which bear witness to the wealth and art of this first great centre of the lagoon. These are the cathedral, the ruined baptistry and the Church of Santa Fosca, the Palazzo del Consiglio and an ancient stone throne called the Sedia di Attila.

CATTEDRALE DI SANTA MARIA ASSUNTA

The cathedral dates from 824 and was partially rebuilt in 1008. The 11th-century bell-tower is one of the tallest of the lagoon. It's well worth a visit to see the stunning mosaics inside.

SANTA FOSCA

Linked to the cathedral by the narthex, this elegantly proportioned church was built in 1100.

Islands. Avoid the "free boat ride" hawke... vaporetto to Murano if you want to tour a Venetian g... across the lagoon, is famed for lacemakers and a v... small island where you can tour a monastery and lit... Michele, the island cemetery of Venice, which is ju... by vaporetto.

olton - The Baby Boo...

The Hard Facts

❑ AIRPORTS

The main airport is Venice Marco Polo, 13 km (8 miles) north of the city. Marco Polo is linked to the city by public bus, once an hour in winter and every half hour in summer. The journey takes about 20 minutes. Airport buses are slightly more expensive but are timed to coincide with arrivals and departures of major airlines. Both buses arrive at Piazzale Roma, from where you board the vaporetto, No. 1 making stops all along the Grand Canal, No. 82 takes a quicker route to San Marco.

Charter flights often use Treviso, 30 km (19 miles) to the north. To get to Venice you have to take bus No. 6 to the centre of Treviso then coach or train to Venice.

❑ BANKS

Opening hours: 8.30 a.m.–1.30 p.m. and 2.35 p.m.–3.35 p.m., Monday to Friday. On local holidays, they close at 11.30 a.m., on other holidays and at weekends they are closed all day.

There is only one cash dispenser in all Venice, in Via XXII Marzo.

❑ CLIMATE

Venice can be damp, chilly and occasionally flooded from November to March, but the rest of the year it is pleasant, reaching a maximum of 28 °C (83 °F) in July and August.

❑ CONSULATES

UK: Palazzo Querini, Dorsoduro 1051
    Tel. 522 72 07

US: Largo Donegani 1, Milan
    Tel. (02) 29 03 51

❑ CURRENCY EXCHANGE

You can change money at banks, at currency exchange offices *(cambio)* or at your hotel. *Cambio* opening hours: 9 a.m.–12.30 p.m. and 3–7.30 p.m. on weekdays; some open on Saturdays in the tourist season (the hours are posted in each office). The exchange office at Santa Lucia Station is also open on Sundays (8.30 a.m.–7 p.m.), and that at Marco-Polo Airport is open every day 9 a.m.–7.30 p.m.

Rates vary from one place to the next; some charge commission.

❑ DRIVING

As Venice is traffic-free you will have to leave your car in one of the multi-level carparks of Piazzale Roma, or on Tronchetto, terminal for the car ferry to the Lido, where driving is allowed.

❑ ELECTRIC CURRENT

Except in the oldest areas of the city, the current is 220 V AC, 50 Hz. Take an adaptor for your appliances.

❑ EMERGENCIES

Police *(carabinieri)*: tel. 112
Emergency services: tel. 113
First Aid: tel. 529 45 16
Ambulance: tel. 523 00 00

Tourists in difficulty can call a help line by dialling 116.

❑ ENTRY REGULATIONS

You will need a valid passport to enter Italy, or, if you are a citizen of an EC country, a National Identity Card. Visas are required only for stays of more than 90 days.

❑ FINDING YOUR WAY

Venice is a small city and you can easily get around on foot. Signposted routes show the principal directions such as Saint Mark's square, the Rial-to, etc. However, as most addresses consist only of the name of the *sestiere* (district) and a number which can run into four figures, it is sometimes difficult to find an exact location. You can buy an "Indicatore anagrafico" which lists all the streets corresponding to the numbers.

It is useful to know the following terms:

calle	street
calletta	narrow street
salizzada	cobbled street
ramo	cul de sac
campo	square
campiello	small square
corte	courtyard
sottoportego	covered passageway
rio	small canal
rio terrà	filled-in canal
riva	quay
fondamenta	quay along canalside
piscina	filled-in arm of the lagoon

❑ GONDOLAS

The official rate is 80,000 L for 6 passengers for 50 minutes, and 40,000 L for every extra 25 minutes. The night tarif, valid from 8 p.m. to 8 a.m., is 100,000 L0. But in any case, first agree the price with the gondolier before you climb aboard.

There are 12 official gondola landing stages *(imbarcadero)*:

Bacino Orseolo, tel. 528 93 16
Calle Vallaresso, tel. 520 61 20
Danieli, Riva Schiavoni, tel. 522 22 54
Ferrovia, S. Lucia, tel. 718 543
Isola Tronchetto, tel. 523 89 19
Piazzale Roma, tel. 522 05 81
Rialto, Riva Carbon, tel. 522 49 04.
S. Marco, tel. 520 06 85
S. Maria del Giglio, tel. 522 20 73
S. Sofia, Pescheria, tel. 522 28 44
S. Tomà, tel. 520 52 75
Trinità, Campo S. Moisé, tel. 523 18 37

❏ LOST PROPERTY

If you lose something on a vaporetto, go to the lost property office:

ACTV, St Angelo stop (N° 9)

Other lost property is held in an office near the Rialto Bridge:

Ufficio all'Economato
Calle Loredam, Ca' Farsetti 4136

❏ POST OFFICE

The Italian postal service handles the mail, money transfers and telegrams. Stamps are also sold in tobacconists and often in hotels.

The main post office in Venice is close to the Rialto, Fontego dei Tedeschi, 80100. Its opening hours are 8.15 a.m.–7 p.m. from Monday to Saturday, with a 24-hour service for telegrams, telex, fax, express and registered post.

Each district also has its post office, open in principal from 8.30 a.m. until 12.30 or 1.30 p.m. The San Marco post office is conveniently situated opposite the Basilica.

❏ PUBLIC HOLIDAYS

January 1	*Capodanno*
January 6	*Befana*
Moveable	*Lunedì di Pasqua*
April 25	*Festa di San Marco*
May 1	*Festa del Lavoro*
August 15	*Ferragosto*
November 1	*Ognissanti*
December 8	*Immacolata Concezione*
December 25	*Natale*
December 26	*Santo Stefano*

Local festivals:

February	Carnival
May	*La Vogalonga:* gondola race on the Sunday after Ascension
July	*Festa del Redentore:* third Sunday of the month
September	*Regata Storica:* Costumed regatta on the Grand Canal, first Sunday of the month
21 November	*Festa della Salute*

❏ PUBLIC TRANSPORT

The **vaporetto**: Routes are frequently modified and it is better to consult the information posted at stops rather than rely on town plans which are often out-of-date. Several lines vary with the season. Line 1, the Accelerato, is in fact the slowest and provides a magnificent cruise on the Grand Canal at little cost.

The **motoscafo** resembles the *vaporetto* but makes fewer stops.

The **motonave** serves longer routes, to the Lido for example. *Motonave* tie up at Stazione Marittima and Riva degli Schiavoni.

The **traghetto**: these ferries cross the Grand Canal at seven different points. Yellow signs indicate the stops.

Tickets: for a single journey the ticket costs 4,500 L; return: 9,000 L (prices March 1997) depending on the distance. A day ticket (15,000 L) is valid on all the lines except 40, 41 and 42). You can buy a 3-day pass for 30,000 L or a 7-day pass for 55,000 L. These passes include the transport of one piece of hand luggage.

The Tourist Office issues a special card for young people between 14 and 29 (called Rolling Venice) which entitles them to various discounts including a *Tre Giorni Giovane* travel pass which is obtainable for 20,000 L at the Piazzale Roma office.

Information:

ACTV, Calle dei Fuseri
Palazzo Regina Vittoria
Open daily 8.30 a.m.–6 p.m. (except Sunday); Saturday 8.30 a.m.–1 p.m.

Piazzale Roma
Open daily 7.30 a.m.–8 p.m.

❏ RELIGIOUS SERVICES

Mass is celebrated in Italian in all the Catholic churches and also in Latin in Saint Mark's at 10 a.m. on Sundays. To hear Gregorian chant, go to Sunday Mass at 11 a.m. at the church of San Giorgio Maggiore.

Synagogue
Ghetto Vecchio, tel. 715 012

Methodist Church Santa Maria Formosa 5170, tel. 523 46 45

Greek Orthodox Church
Ponte dei Greci 3412, tel. 522 54 46

Saint George's Anglican Church
Campo San Vio 870, tel. 520 05 71

Church of Jesus Christ of Latterday Saints; Via Castellana 124/C Zelarin, tel. 90 81 81

❏ TAXIS
The *taxi acquei* or *motoscafi di nolo* (water taxis) wait at a dozen stations. The prices are fixed, but it's always better to come to an agreement with the driver before you set off, as some of them tend to exaggerate. In the historic centre, the rate is fixed at 30,000 L for the first seven minutes, then 500 L for every following 15 seconds. But there are numerous extras for luggage, night service, holidays, etc.
Central telephone (24-hour service): 522 23 03

❏ TELEPHONE
The telephone boxes which are scattered throughout the city require 200 L coins, phonecards or tokens *(gettoni)*. You can buy phonecards and tokens at post offices, bars, tobacconists, some newspaper kiosks, the headquarters for Italian telecommunications (TELECOM) and at the station. It is nevertheless easier to call from a public telephone centre where you pay at the counter after the call is completed. These centres are next to the central post office near the Rialto, at Ruga Vecchia San Giovanni, at Santa Lucia Station and at TELECOM, Piazzale Roma.

The outgoing international code is 00. Then dial the country code (UK 44; USA and Canada 1, Australia 61, New Zealand 64) and the area code without the initial zero, followed by the local number.
For enquiries, dial 10.

❏ TIPPING
Service charges are included in restaurants, but you can leave a few extra coins to show appreciation. It is usual to tip the hotel porter, the doorman or anyone else who does you a small service.

❏ TOURIST OFFICES
At the ATP offices you can pick up useful free brochures and maps. *Un Ospite di Venezia*, available in hotels, is full of information on everything that's going on: cultural, religious and sporting events, timetables, rates for public and private services, addresses of duty pharmacies.
The APT offices are at:
Giardinetti Reali, Palazzetto Selva
Tel. 522 63 56

Stazione Santa Lucia
Tel. 529 87 27

❏ WATER
Tap water is safe to drink, and there are drinking fountains all over the city. If ever the water is *not* fit for drinking it is marked with a sign: *Acqua non potabile*.

59

1		P.le Roma - Ferrovia - Canal Grande - Lido
3		Tronchetto - Canal Grande - S.Zaccaria -Tronchetto
4		S.Zaccaria - Canal Grande - Tronchetto - S.Zaccaria
6		S.Zaccaria - Lido
10		Venetia - Ospedali lagunari
20		Venetia - Ospedali lagunari
12		Venezia - Burano - Torcello
13		Venezia -S.Erasmo -Treporti
14		Venezia - Punta Sabbioni - Treporti - Burano - Torcello
14		Venezia - Punta Sabbioni
16		Venezia - Fusina
17		Trasporto automezzi Venezia - Lido
23		S.Zaccaria - S.Elena - Murano - Fondamente Nove - S.Zaccaria
52		Lido - S.Zaccaria - Zattere - P.le Roma - Ferrovia - F.te Nove - Murano
52		P.le Roma - Giudecca - S Zaccaria - F.te Nove - Murano
82		S.Zaccaria - S.Marco - Canal Grande - Tronchetto - Giudecca - S.Zaccaria - Lido

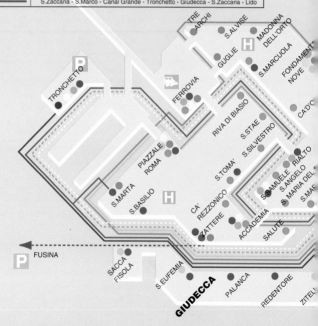

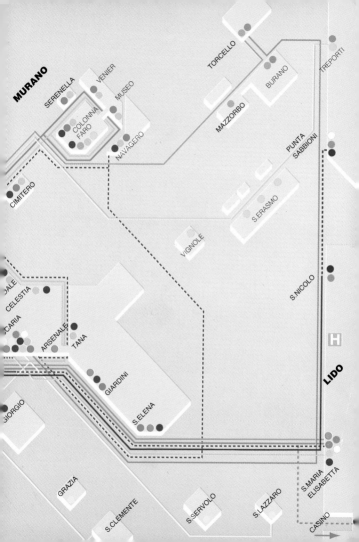

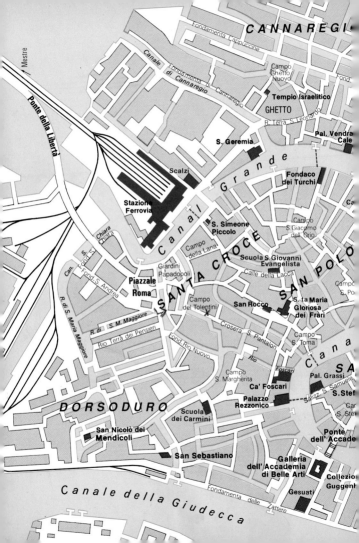

CANNAREGI[O]

Fondamenta Cappuccine

Canale di Cannaregio

Fondamenta di Cannaregio

Mestre

Ponte della Libertà

Campo Ghetto Nuovo

Fond

Tempio Israelitico

GHETTO

R. Terra S. Leonardo

S. Geremia

Pal. Vendra Cale

Scalzi

Canal Grande

Fondaco dei Turchi

Ca

Stazione Ferrovia

S. Simeone Piccolo

SANTA CROCE

Campo S. Giacomo dell'Orio

Chiara Chiata

Campo della Lana

Scuola S. Giovanni Evangelista

Calle della Lacca

SAN POLO

Giardini Papadopoli

Cam S. Po

Cant.

Fond. S. Andrea

Piazzale Roma

Campo del Tolentini

San Rocco

S. ta Maria Gloriosa dei Frari

R. di S. Maria Maggiore

R. di S.M. Maggiore

Crosera S. Pantalon

Campo S. Toma

Rio Terrà dei Pensieri

Fond. Rio Nuovo

Rio

Cana

DORSODURO

Campo S. Margherita

Foscari

Pal. Grassi

SA

Ca' Foscari

Salizz. S. Samuele

S. Stef

Scuola dei Carmini

Palazzo Rezzonico

Cam S. Ste

San Nicolò dei Mendicoli

Ponte dell'Accade

San Sebastiano

Galleria dell'Accademia di Belle Arti

Collezio Guggent

Gesuati

Canale della Giudecca

Fondamenta delle Zattere

General editor:	Barbara Ender-Jones
Research:	Francesca Grazzi and Farid Rahimi
Text:	Jack Altman and Judith Farr
Layout:	Dominique Michellod and André Misteli
Photography:	Claude Huber
Maps:	Falk-Verlag, Hamburg

Printed in Switzerland

The Italian Way

Buon giorno!
Hello!

Buon giorno!   *Hello!*

Wherever you travel in Italy, people appreciate your greeting them with a *"buon giorno"* (literally "good day") or *"buona sera"* ("good evening"). Save *"buona notte"* ("good night") for when you're off to bed.

Add *"come sta?"* ("how are you?") and your Italian had better be good enough to understand the answer. With luck, your accent will give you away and the Italians will be kind enough just to answer *"bene, grazie"* ("well, thank you") and not give you a rundown on their ailments and tax problems. If they are the first to ask, reply: *"Bene, grazie"* and add: *"E lei?"* ("And you?"). The proper response to *"grazie"* by itself is *"prego"* ("don't mention it"). Make your way through a crowded bus with a polite *"Permesso"* ("May I?").

Men and women shake hands on a first meeting. With a woman, once you've struck up a friendship, exchange a light kiss on each cheek, usually an airy affair to avoid lipstick marks or misunderstandings. Down south, men commonly exchange a Godfatherly bear-hug. It's quite harmless.

And the whole world already knows how to say "good bye": *"Ciao!"* or *"Arrivederci"*.

Good morning/ afternoon.	Buon giorno.	bwohn JOHR-noh
Good evening.	Buona sera.	BWOH-nah SEH-rah
Good night.	Buona notte.	BWOH-nah NOHT-teh
Goodbye.	Arrivederci.	ahr-ree-veh-DEHR-chee
See you later.	A più tardi.	ah pyoo TAHR-dee
Hi!/Bye!	Ciao!	CHAA-oh
Yes/No.	Sì/No.	see/noh
Maybe.	Forse.	FOHR-seh
That's fine/Okay.	D'accordo.	dah-KOHR-doh
That's right!	Va bene.	vah BEH-neh

Please.	Per favore.	pehr fah-VAW-reh
Thank you/Thanks.	Grazie.	GRAA-tsyeh
Thank you very much.	Tante grazie.	TAHN-teh GRAA-tsyeh
You're welcome.	Prego.	PREH-goh
Nice to meet you.	Molto lieto.	MOHL-toh LYEH-toh
How are you?	Come sta?	KAW-meh stah
Well, thanks.	Bene, grazie.	BEH-neh, GRAA-tsyeh
And you?	E lei?	eh lay
Pardon me.	Mi scusi.	mee SKOO-zee
I'm sorry.	Mi dispiace.	mee dee-SPYAA-cheh
Don't mention it.	Non c'è di che.	nohn cheh dee keh
Excuse me…	Scusi…	SKOO-zee
My name is…	Mi chiamo…	mee KYAA-moh
I don't understand.	Non capisco.	nohn kah-PEE-skoh
Slowly, please.	Parli piano.	PAHR-lee PYAA-noh
Could you say that again?	Può ripetere, per favore?	pwoh ree-PEH-teh-reh, pehr fah-VAW-reh
Do you speak English?	Parla inglese?	PAHR-lah eeng-GLEH-zeh
I don't speak much Italian.	Non parlo bene l'italiano.	nohn PAHR-loh BEH-neh lee-tah-LYAA-noh
Please write it down.	Per favore, me lo scriva.	pehr fah-VAW-reh, meh loh SKREE-vah
I understand.	Capisco.	kah-PEE-skoh
Let's go.	Andiamo.	ahn-DYAA-moh

Don't be shy. To help you with your spoken Italian we provide a very simple transcription alongside the phrases. You may not and up sounding like a native speaker but people will be pleased to hear you trying.

Taxi! Taxi!

Official metered yellow cabs line up at railway stations or outside major hotels, only rarely hailed on the move. Beware of pirate drivers, identifiable by the fact that *they* approach you. Unauthorized cars are called in Italian *abusivi*, which says it all. Expect legitimate extras on the meter price, particularly at night, with bags or going to the airport—rates posted in the vehicle. Add a 10 per cent tip.

Public transport. Services for the bus *(autobus)* vary— good in Florence and Milan, overcrowded in Rome and Naples. The water-bus in Venice *(vaporetto* or smaller, faster *motoscafo)* is best of all. The bus stop *(fermata)* displays bus-number and route served. For cheaper fares, buy a book of tickets *(blochetto di biglietti)* at news-stands or tobacconists. Get on through the door marked *"Salita"* and off at the exit marked *"Uscita"*. Subway trains, *Metro(politano)*, operate in Milan and Rome, tickets interchangeable with the bus system.

Trains. Besides the luxury international *EuroCity*, (EC) and the *Intercity* (IC) there's the *Rapido*, faster than the *Espresso*, which is crowded but faster than the *Diretto*. The *Locale* seems to stop for anyone who cares to whistle it down.

Taxi, please!	Taxi!	TAH-ksee
Are you free?	È libero?	eh LEE-beh-roh
Hotel Paradiso, please.	Hotel Paradiso, per favore.	oh-TEHL pah-rah-DEE-zoh, pehr fah-VAW-reh
To the airport/the station, please.	All'aeroporto/alla stazione, per favore.	ahl-lah-eh-roh-POHR-toh/ AHL-lah stah-TSYAW-neh, pehr fah-VAW-reh
I'm in a hurry.	Ho fretta.	oh FREHT-tah
Please stop here.	Si fermi qui.	see FEHR-mee kwee

Please wait for me.	Aspetti un momento, per favore.	ah-SPEHT-tee oon moh-MEHN-toh, pehr fah-VAW-reh
How much is it?	Quant'è?	kwahn-TEH
Keep the change.	Tenga il resto.	TEHNG-gah eel REH-stoh
Where is the metro, please?	Dov'è il metrò, per favore?	daw-VEH eel meh-TROH, pehr fah-VAW-reh
A book of tickets, please.	Un blocchetto di biglietti, per favore.	oon blohk-KEHT-toh dee bee-LYEHT-tee, pehr fah-VAW-reh
one-way	andata	ahn-DAA-tah
round-trip	andata e ritorno	ahn-DAA-tah eh ree-TOHR-noh
first class	prima classe	PREE-mah KLAHS-seh
second class	seconda classe	seh-KOHN-dah KLAHS-seh
platform	binario	bee-NAA-ryoh
toilets	gabinetti	gah-bee-NEHT-tee
Is this seat free?	È libero questo posto?	eh LEE-beh-roh KWEH-stoh POH-stoh

False Friends: Many Italian words look like direct equivalents of English words, but you could be very wrong:

camera	room
conveniente	cheap, inexpensive
fresco	cool
incidente	accident
libreria	bookstore
magazzino	warehouse
moneta	coins, change
morbido	soft
pila	battery (transistor, flashlight)
slip	underpants

Direttore *Manager*

Your hotel lobby is where you first learn how much Italians like their titles. You'll get better service if you call the hall-porter or bell-captain *portiere,* as opposed to *facchino* (baggage porter or bellhop). Upstairs, the room maid is *cameriera.* Hotel tipping also has its fine distinctions: on the spot to porters for carrying bags or other incidental services, but a lump sum to room maids at the end of the stay.

Ratings for the hotel *(hotel* or *albergo)* range from luxury five-star to rudimentary one-star. Expect in-house laundry and dry-cleaning services only from three-star and better. Breakfast is generally optional but in high season, resort hotels often insist on at least half-board. Boarding houses *(pensione)* have a separate rating-system from very comfortable, with good family cooking, to modest, providing just basic services. Distinguish between humble accommodation in monasteries run by monks and the often luxurious amenities of converted monasteries run by hoteliers.

If you have checked out of your hotel, you can still take a *siesta* and bath in a low-price day hotel *(albergo diurno),* usually close to the main railway station.

I've a reservation	Ho fatto una prenotazione	oh FAHT-toh oo-nah preh-noh-ta-TSYAW-neh
Here's the confirmation/voucher.	Ecco la conferma, il buono.	EHK-koh lah kohn-FEHR-mah/eel BWAW-noh
a single room	una camera singola	OO-nah KAA-meh-rah SEENG-goh-lah
a double	una camera doppia	OO-nah KAA-meh-rah DOHP-pyah
twin beds	letti gemelli	LEHT-tee jeh-MEHL-lee
double bed	letto matrimoniale	LEHT-toh mah-tree-moh-NYAA-leh
with a bath/shower	con bagno/doccia	kohn BAH-nyoh/DOHT-chah

My key, please.	La mia chiave, per favore.	lah MEE-ah KYAA-veh, pehr fah-VAW-reh
Is there mail for me?	C'è posta per me?	cheh POH-stah pehr meh
I need:	Ho bisogno di:	oh bee-ZAW-nyoh dee
hangers	grucce	GROOT-che
soap	una saponetta	OO-nah sah-poh-NEHT-tah
a blanket	una coperta	OO-nah koh-PEHR-tah
an (extra) pillow	un guanciale (in più)	oon gwahn-CHAA-leh (een pyoo)
This is for the laundry.	Questo è da lavare.	KWEH-stoh eh dah lah-VAA-reh
These are clothes to be cleaned/ pressed.	Questi sono vestiti da pulire/ stirare.	KWEH-stee SAW-noh veh-STEE-tee dah poo-LEE-reh/stee-RAA-reh
Urgently.	È urgente.	eh oor-JEHN-teh
I'm checking out.	Lascio l'albergo.	LAHSH-shoh lahl-BEHR-goh
I'd like to pay by credit card	Vorrei pagare con la mia carta di credito.	vohr-RAY pah-GAA-reh kohn lah MEE-ah KAHR-tah dee KREH-dee-toh

Notices. The meaning of some signs you'll see:

Chiuso	Closed
Entrata (Ingresso)	Entrance
Guasto	Out of order
Signore (or Donne)	Ladies
Signori (or Uomini)	Gentlemen
Uscita	Exit
Vietato	Forbidden
Vietato fumare	No smoking

Buon appetito! *Enjoy your meal!*

The advantage of the ordinary *trattoria* restaurant over the more formal (and higher priced) establishment known as a *ristorante* is usually apparent as you walk in. Much of the day's "menu" is appetizingly laid out on a long table or refrigerated counter. The display includes not only cold starters *(antipasti)* but also fish *(pesce)* or other seafood *(frutti di mare)* and even cuts of meat *(carne)*. State your cooking preference: *alla griglia* (grilled), *fritto* (fried) or *al forno* (baked).

The *pasta* of course is off in the kitchen, but comes these days in literally hundreds of different shapes and sizes—manufacturers even have architects to design new forms.

At midday, you may prefer the stand-up bar known as *tavola calda*, where you can get sandwiches and a hot or cold dish at the counter. Better than fast-food is the *panino ripieno*, a bread roll stuffed with cold meats, sausage, salad or cheese—your personal choice from the counter-display—the original of the American "submarine".

I'm hungry/thirsty.	Ho fame/sete.	oh FAA-meh/SEH-teh
A table for two, please.	Un tavolo per due, per favore.	oon TAA-voh-loh pehr DOO-eh, pehr fa-VAW-reh
The menu, please.	Il menù, per favore.	eel meh-NOO, pehr fah-VAW-reh
The fixed menu, please.	Il menú fisso, per favore.	eel meh-NOO FEES-soh, pehr fah-VAW-reh
I'm a vegetarian.	Sono vegetariano(a).	SAW-noh veh-jeh-tah-RYAA-noh(ah)
A glass of water, please.	Un bicchiere d'acqua, per favore.	oon-beek-KYEH-reh DAHK-kwah, pehr fah-VAW-reh
I'd like a beer	Vorrei una birra.	vohr-RAY oo-nah BEER-rah.

The wine list, please.	La carte dei vini, per favore.	lah KAHR-tah day VEE-nee, pehr fah-VAW-reh
A bottle of red/white/rosé wine.	Una bottiglia di vino rosso/bianco/rosato.	oo-nah boht-TEE-lyah dee VEE-noh ROHS-soh/BYANG-koh/roh-ZAA-toh
beef	manzo	MAHN-dzoh
bread	pane	PAA-neh
butter	burro	BOOR-roh
cheese	formaggio	fohr-MAHD-joh
chicken	pollo	POHL-loh
coffee	caffè	kahf-FEH
fish	pesce	PEHSH-sheh
fruit juice	succo di frutta	SOOK-koh dee FROOT-tah
ice cream	gelato	jeh-LAA-toh
meat	carne	KAHR-neh
milk	latte	LAHT-teh
mineral water (carbonated/flat)	acqua minerale (gasata/naturale)	AHK-kwah mee-neh-RAA-leh (gah-ZAA-tah/nah-too-RAA-leh)
mustard	senape	SEH-nah-peh
pork	maiale	mah-YAA-leh
salt and pepper	sale e pepe	SAA-leh eh PEH-peh
tea	tè	teh
vegetables	verdura	vehr-DOO-rah
The check, please.	Il conto, per favore.	eel KOHN-toh, pehr fah-VAW-reh

You and you. There are several ways of saying "you" in Italian. *Tu* (plural *voi*) is famliar, used for children, friends, family. *Lei* (plural *loro*) is polite, for people you don't know well. And if you meet the person of your dreams, "I love you" is *Ti amo*.

Pronto! Chi parla?
Hello, who's speaking?

Note that on the telephone, "Hello" in Italian is not *Buon giorno* but *"Pronto!"* It means literally that the caller is "ready" to speak, a national characteristic. If you are answering the phone, in all likelihood, your next phrase should be *"Parla inglese?"* ("Do you speak English?") If the answer is *"No"*, try *"Qui parla..."* ("This is ... speaking").

In recent years, Italy has greatly modernized and streamlined its telephone network, hiving it off from the national post office as the separate Telecom company. For public telephones *(cabina telefonica)*, electronic telephone cards are universally replacing coins. The old slotted token *(gettone)* is fast becoming a collector's item, but is still in use at some bars, cafés and tobacconists. In any case, it will be cheaper using public telephones than paying the hotel's surcharge.

To call the U.S. and Canada direct, dial 001. For the U.K., the country code is 0044.

1 uno	6 sei	11 undici	16 sedici
2 due	7 sette	12 dodici	17 diciassette
3 tre	8 otto	13 tredici	18 diciotto
4 quattro	9 nove	14 quattordici	19 diciannove
5 cinque	10 dieci	15 quindici	20 venti

May I use this phone?	Posso usare questo telefono?	POHS-soh oo-ZAA-reh KWEH-stoh teh-LEH-foh-noh
Can I reverse the charges?	Posso telefonare a carico del destinatario?	POHS-soh teh-leh-foh-NAA-reh ah KAA-ree-koh dehl deh-stee-nah-TOH-ryoh
Wrong number.	Numero sbagliato.	NOO-meh-roh zbah-LYAA-toh

Speak more slowly, please.	Parli più piano, per favore.	PAHR-lee pyoo PYAA-noh, pehr fah-VAW-reh
Could you take a message?	Può prendere un messaggio?	pwoh PREHN-deh-reh oon mehs-SAHD-joh
My number is…	Il mio numero è il…	eel MEE-oh NOO-meh-roh eh eel
My room number is…	Il mio numero di camera è il…	eel MEE-oh NOO-meh-roh dee KAA-meh-rah eh eel
Do you sell stamps?	Avete dei francobolli?	ah-VEH-teh day frahng-koh-BOHL-lee
How much is it to Great Britain/ the United States?	Quanto è per la Gran Bretagna/ gli Stati Uniti?	KWAHN-toh eh pehr lah grahn breh-TAH-nyah/ lyee STAA-tee oo-NEE-tee
I'd like to mail this parcel.	Vorrei spedire questo pacco.	vohr-RAY speh-DEE-reh KWEH-sto PAHK-koh
Can I send a fax?	Posso mandare un fax?	POHS-soh mahn-DAA-reh oon fahks
Can I make a photocopy here?	Posso fare una fotocopia qui?	POHS-soh FAA-reh OO-nah foh-toh-KAW-pyah kwee
Where's the mailbox?	Dov'è la cassetta delle lettere?	daw-VEH lah kahs-SEHT-tah DEHL-leh LEHT-teh-reh
registered letter	lettera raccomandata	LEHT-teh-rah rahk-kohm-mahn-DAA-tah
air mail	via aerea	VEE-ah ah-EH-reh-ah
postcard	cartolina postale	kahr-toh-LEE-nah poh-STAA-leh

Happy Talk: Build up your vocabulary with a few useful, cheery adjectives: *simpatico* (charming), *splendido* (magnificient), *fantastico* (terrific), *formidabile* (tremendous).

Quanto? How much?

The *lira* (plural: *lire*) is the national unit of currency. Coins come in denominations of 500, 200, 100, 50, 20, 10 and 5 lire, but these days you rarely see anything below 50 *lire*. If you have coin change coming to you at motorway tollbooths, you may even be "paid" with sweets (candy). Biggest banknote is 100,000, then 50,000, 10,000 and 5,000 *lire,* with 2,000 and 1,000 *lire* gradually dropping out of circulation. Prices are often written without the last three zeros.

The better exchange rate you get at the bank compared with the hotel is offset by the amount of time spent waiting in line, often one to make the initial transaction and another to collect the cash. Have your passport with you. In most places, banks are open Monday to Friday, 8.30 a.m. to 1.30 p.m. and another hour in mid-afternoon. Railway station and airport currency exchange offices stay open longer, and weekends as well. Most convenient of all are the automatic cash dispensers for international credit cards (at stations and main tourist centres), but the commission rate is high.

currency exchange	cambio	KAHM-byoh
Where can I change money?	Dove posso cambiare del denaro?	DAW-veh POHS-soh kahm-BYAA-reh dehl deh-NAA-roh
Can you cash a traveler's check?	Può incassare un traveller's check?	pwoh een-kahs-SAA-reh oon "traveller's check"
I want to change dollars/pounds.	Voglio cambiare dei dollari/ delle sterline.	VOH-lyoh kahm-BYAA-reh day DOHL-lah-ree/ DEHL-leh stehr-LEE-neh

English	Italian	Pronunciation
Will this credit card do?	Accetta questa carta di credito?	aht-CHEHT-tah KWEH-stah KAHR-tah dee KREH-dee-toh
Can you help me?	Può aiutarmi?	pwoh ah-yoo-TAAR-mee
Just looking…	Sto solo guardando…	stoh SAW-loh gwahr-DAHN-doh
How much is this?	Quant'è?	kwahn-TEH
cheap	buon mercato	bwohn mehr-KAA-toh
expensive	caro	KAA-roh
Can I try it on?	Posso provarlo?	POHS-soh proh-VAHR-loh
I don't know the European sizes.	Non conosco le taglie europee.	nohn koh-NOH-skoh leh TAA-lyeh eh-oo-roh-PEH-eh
I'll think about it.	Voglio pensarci.	VOH-lyoh pehn-SAHR-chee
I'll buy it.	Lo prendo.	loh PREHN-doh
It's a gift.	È un regalo.	eh oon reh-GAA-loh
A receipt, please.	Una ricevuta, per favore.	OO-nah ree-cheh-VOO-tah, pehr fah-VAW-reh
antique shop	antiquario	ahn-tee-KWAA-ryoh
bakery	panetteria	pah-neht-teh-REE-ah
drugstore	farmacia	fahr-mah-CHEE-ah
flea market	mercato delle pulci	mehr-KAA-toh DEHL-leh POOL-chee
jewellery store	gioielleria	joh-yehl-leh-REE-ah
pastry shop	pasticceria	pah-steet-cheh-REE-ah
supermarket	supermercato	soo-pehr-mehr-KAA-toh

Question mark. To ask a question in Italian, all you have to do is change the inflexion of your voice, lifting it towards the end of the sentence:

It's far away.	**È lontano.**
It's far?	**È lontano**?

Aiuto! *Help!*

The best planned vacation may sometimes be spoiled—by a stomach upset or something of the sort. Too much sun, too much Chianti in the middle of the day and you'll be looking around for the drugstore *(farmacia)*. One of them is open somewhere in town, even nights and weekends. Most often, it's located near the main railway station.

If you're prone to something that needs special medication, take a supply from home since, as good as most Italian medicine is, you may not be able to find precisely the same prescription on the spot. The emergency number to dial for an ambulance is **113**.

Safety First. No need to be paranoid, but it's silly to take pointless risks. The precautions are simple. Leave your valuables in the hotel's safe *(cassaforte)* and carry only as much cash as you need. Keep your passport separate from your traveller's cheques and credit cards. If you've rented a car, don't park it with bags visible on the seats.

Police come in two kinds: *Vigili Urbani* (municipal police) in navy blue uniforms or all white in summer; and *Carabinieri* in brown or black, handling major crimes and street-demonstrations. Emergency number (as for ambulances): **113**

I don't feel well.	**Non mi sento bene.**	nohn mee SEHN-toh BEH-neh
Where is a drugstore?	**Dov'è una farmacia?**	daw-VEH OO-nah fahr-mah-CHEE-ah
an upset stomach	**un'indigestione**	oon-een-dee-jeh-STYAW-neh
an injury	**una ferita**	OO-nah feh-REE-tah

| toothache | mal di denti | mahl dee DEHN-tee |
| headache | mal di testa | mahl dee TEH-stah |

I feel pain…	Mi fa male…	mee fah MAA-leh
… in my leg	… la gamba	lah GAHM-bah
… in my arm	… il braccio	eel BRAH-choh
… in my stomach	… lo stomaco	loh STOM-mah-koh
… in my chest	… il petto	eel PEHT-toh
I am bleeding.	Perdo sangue.	PEHR-doh SANG-gweh
I need a doctor.	Ho bisogno di un dottore.	oh bee-ZAW-nyoh dee oon doht-TAW-reh
I feel dizzy.	Ho le vertigini.	oh leh vehr-TEE-jee-nee

| Can you give me a prescription? | Può darmi una ricetta? | pwoh DAHR-mee OO-nah ree-CHEHT-tah |

Help!	Aiuto!	ah-YOO-toh
Stop thief!	Al ladro!	ahl LAA-droh
Leave me alone.	Mi lasci in pace.	mee LASH-shee een PAA-cheh

| I've lost my wallet/ passport. | Ho perso il portafogli/ il passaporto. | oh PEHR-soh eel pohr-tah-FAW-lyee/ eel pahs-sah-POHR-toh |

| My credit cards have been stolen. | Mi hanno rubato le carte di credito. | mee AHN-noh roo-BAA-toh leh KAHR-teh dee KREH-dee-toh |

I'm lost.	Mi sono perso.	mee SAW-noh PEHR-soh
Where's the police station/the hospital?	Dov'è la polizia/ l'ospedale?	daw-VEH lah poh-lee-TSEE-ah/ loh-speh-DAA-leh
I have been assaulted.	Sono stato aggredito.	SAW-noh STAA-to ahg-greh-DEE-toh

| witness | testimone | tes-tee-MOH-neh |
| lawyer | avvocato | av-voh-KAH-toh |

THE ITALIAN WAY: INDEX

Signs Around Town:

Al completo	Full/No vacancies
Ascensore	Lift/Elevator
Cassa	Cashier
Chiuso	Closed
Pedoni	Pedestrians
Pintura fresca	Wet paint
Spingere	Push
Saldi/Svendite	Sale
Suonare, per favore	Please ring the bell
Uscita di sicurezza	Emergency exit
Tirare	Pull

Italian State Tourist Office (ENIT)

UK: 1 Princes Street, London WIR 8 AY.
 Tel: (0171) 408 1254.   Fax: (0171) 493 6695.
USA: Suite 1565, 630 Fifth Avenue, New York, NY 10111.
 Tel: (212) 245 4822.   Fax: (212) 586 9249.
Canada: Suite 1914, 1 place de Ville Marie, Montréal, Quebec H3B 2C3
 Tel: (514) 866 7667.   Fax: (514) 392 1429.

JPM Publications SA • *Specialists in customized guides*

12, avenue William-Fraisse, 1006 Lausanne, Switzerland
Copyright © 1996 JPM Publications SA – Printed in Switzerland – 8001 00 1

9/703